pure**awareness**

Five Simple Techniques for Experiencing Your Essential Nature

By
Tom Stone

Pure Awareness

Five Simple Techniques for Experiencing Your Essential Nature

Published by:

Great Life Technologies, LLC

7040 Avenida Encinas, Suite 104 #380

Carlsbad, CA 92011

(619-557-2700

www.greatlifetechnologies.com

Copyright © 2007 by Tom Stone

Magma font use throughout this book designed by Sumner Stone

www.stonetypefoundry.com

To my wonderful wife

Lynda

Acknowledgments

My heart felt thanks to all those who have contributed to my personal journey that has lead to the insights I am sharing here. The teachers and life experiences are too numerous to mention as every life experience has contributed in some way or another to bringing me to the knowledge of these wonderful Pure Awareness Techniques.

First I would like to give thanks for my beautiful daughters Sharma and Serenity, for their love and for the great enrichment, insight and wisdom that having them in my life has brought me.

I would like to express my deep appreciation to the team of people who provided valuable suggestions and feedback about the book and helped with the reviewing and editing of the manuscript including Magi Speelpenning, Steve Straus, Patricia Coleman, Gracia Wenzel, and Susan White. I'm also very grateful to Michelle LaPrise for her ideas and contributions.

I have an especially deep gratitude to Michael Stratford for his contribution to the special application of the GAP technique and his delightful collaboration in teaching Core Dynamics Coach Training with me. I am also deeply grateful for the wonderful support of my work from Leon Weiner, Tony Soto, Bob Brock, Wendy Down, Christian Mickelson and Drew Rozell.

I am particularly grateful to all of my clients, seminar and training program participants, the Core Dynamics Coaches and Teachers, the WaveMaker Coaches and Human Software Engineers who have so whole heartedly embraced this work and who have provided an environment in which these techniques could be refined and perfected over the years. It is these pioneers of Human Software Engineering who are really propagating this work in the world. To all of you I offer my deepest gratitude.

And I am grateful to you dear reader for opening these pages and for coming to this moment in your life in which you are on the threshold of learning some of the most important knowledge that you may ever come to know. May you use and enjoy these precious Pure Awareness techniques and live and enjoy the totality of who and what you really are for the rest of your life!

Tom Stone
June 2007

Table of Contents

Preface

What you are about to learn will very likely be some of the most profound and important tools that you ever learn in your life. These simple techniques can liberate you from the grip of emotion. They can bring you out of suffering. They can vaporize problems that you thought couldn't be solved. They can give you the experience of the answer to the question of who and what you really are. They can connect you to your essential nature and to the essence of everything in the universe.

The Pure Awareness Techniques can bring you the direct experience of what quantum physics calls the Unified Field. They can help you to live in the "zone" all the time. They can bring you out of inner conflicts and illusions. They can help you to easily break habits that you want to break. They can save you from the grip of addictive behavior. They can bring you deep and lasting fulfillment that is more precious than any other accomplishment you can have in your life.

And they are simple, easy to learn and easy to practice.

And it doesn't take long to begin to liberate yourself from fear, anger, guilt, regret, resentment, depression, anxiety, worry, nervousness, and suffering, and to begin to experience more joy, fulfillment, success and happiness in your life than every before.

Those are big promises but they are easy to realize. It's not by reading the book that this will happen but by learning and practicing the techniques presented here. You only have to remember to use them. These five simple techniques provide you with the quickest way that I have found to free yourself from suffering and problems. All you have to do is learn and practice the Five Pure Awareness Techniques in this simple book and all of this and more will be yours.

Enjoy Pure Awareness for it is the reality of what you truly are,

Tom Stone
June, 2007
Carlsbad, California

What is Pure Awareness?

Pure Awareness is very simple. It is that with which you experience everything. It is that attribute of you that is your awakeness, your aliveness. It is the screen of your mind upon which fall all of your thoughts and perceptions. It is your consciousness.

It is so simple that we don't notice that it is there. Because Pure Awareness is not an object of experience itself and is only in the background we don't normally notice that it is there. It's too simple, too silent, too... uninteresting!

So why have a book about Pure Awareness if it's so simple and uninteresting? Because although most people are completely unaware that they have something called Pure Awareness within them it is absolutely the most important part of everyone. In fact it is our essential nature. It is our very aliveness. It is what makes us alive and able to perceive and think and experience life.

Throughout recorded history, the experience of Pure Awareness has been a great spiritual quest for untold thousands of seekers of truth. Meditation and other spiritual practices aspire to attain the direct experience of Pure Awareness. It goes by many names in the spiritual seeking circles such as Samadhi, Satori, Transcendental Consciousness, the Source, the Now, the Presence, the Absolute, Universality, Wholeness, Enlightenment! The transcendentalist Ralph Waldo Emerson, Henry David Thoreau, Margaret Fuller and others attempted to describe it in their writings. Some authors on the subject describe having an experience of Pure Awareness only to lose it and then struggle for years trying their hardest to capture the experience yet again.

In the spiritual traditions of the world people dedicate their lives to the pursuit of the experience of Pure Awareness and spend countless hours, days, years, and— according to some beliefs—lifetimes pursuing it. There are many disparate notions about what Pure Awareness is. And there have been a myriad of diverse practices, some of which are quite austere, that people have pursued for many years in the faint hope of catching a glimpse of Pure Awareness.

And yet, as you will soon see, to experience Pure Awareness is so incredibly simple that all that is needed is to look in the right place and there it is. Anyone can do this and have the experience in moments. It's that easy.

Intellectual Understanding vs. Direct Experience

There are two aspects to truly knowing anything. One is direct experience and the other is intellectual understanding. Of the two, direct experience really has to come first because without it you don't really have any true basis of understanding what something is.

For example, if you asked someone who had never tasted a strawberry what one tastes like, they would have to say they didn't know. And if you tried to describe the taste of a strawberry to them you would say, well it's sweet, and tart, and juicy, the seeds can be a little bit crunchy, it tastes like a... strawberry! Would any description in words really be able to help them truly know what a strawberry tastes like without having tasted one? Of course not! You have to have the direct experience of tasting a strawberry in order to know what it is. Then and only then does the description begin to make sense.

So true understanding is dependent upon direct experience. It is only possible to know what something truly is through directly experiencing it ourselves, not through having an intellectual understanding of it.

Experience Pure Awareness Right Now

In order for this book to make sense to you it will be necessary for you to experience Pure Awareness directly before we go too far. So I highly recommend that you do one of two things. One is to go to the web page listed below where there is an audio recording of my guiding you through the experience of the GAP technique. The web page is located at - http://greatlifetechnologies.com/GAP.html

Type this URL into your web browser and when you access the page you can listen to the recording in which I guide you to experience Pure Awareness within yourself. It is quite easy and it only takes a few minutes.

The other is to have someone read the steps of experiencing the GAP technique to you from the guided steps section which follows shortly. It is much easier to have someone read the steps to you than trying to do it yourself from the guidelines in the book as the technique is best done with your eyes closed.

How to do the "GAP" Pure Awareness Technique

Experience the gap between thoughts

The purpose of this exercise is to shift the attention from an outward direction to an inward direction so that it is possible to experience the essential nature of awareness itself. Recent scientific research in neuroscience confirms that there are periods of inactivity in the brain that correspond to the gaps between thoughts.

To start this technique, ask the person to sit quietly and close their eyes. Wait for about half a minute to let them simply experience what it is like to sit with their eyes closed. Then you can say the following: "Notice that with your eyes closed you experience several kinds of things. You hear my voice, you may notice feeling your body sitting in a chair, you may notice other noises or sensations, and you will notice that there are thoughts coming to you."

"Notice that the thoughts are like speaking; They don't come in one long run-on sentence. There are pauses or gaps (however brief) in between the thoughts."

"Allow yourself to simply notice the gap in between the thoughts." [Now wait for about half a minute]. "Notice that the gaps between thoughts are truly empty. There is nothing there. It's just pure awareness without the awareness of anything else. It is lively but there is no object of experience."

"Another way to directly experience this nothingness of Pure Awareness is to simply notice that the thoughts that you experience in your mind are occurring in a background of silence. Some people find it easier to just shift their attention from noticing the activity of the thoughts to noticing the silent background in which the thoughts are occurring.

"As you notice the silent background in which the thoughts are occurring, you will notice that you can be aware of it even while the thoughts are coming and going. Allow yourself to simply favor noticing that silent background. Immerse yourself in that silence. [Wait about one minute]

If you find that you have become absorbed in thinking, at the moment when you notice this, simply bring your attention back to the gap between the thoughts." [Wait one to two minutes here.]

5

Then say "Okay. When you're ready, open your eyes."

What did you experience? What was it like? What are the attributes of Pure Awareness?

You may get responses such as: It's quiet. It's peaceful. It's expansive. It's pleasant, relaxing. It's very ... nice.

When I use the term Pure Awareness, do you now know from this experience what Pure Awareness is?

Now that you have experienced your own Pure Awareness, it is easy to notice that the Pure Awareness is always there, lively in the background, even with your eyes open and with the activity of experiencing the objects of the senses. Can you still feel the presence of the Pure Awareness? Is there anything lacking in the experience of that pure awareness? Is there anything that you could not do from this place? Is there any sense of feeling needy while you are aware of Pure Awareness?

If you aren't sure whether you had a clear experience of Pure Awareness or not, this is to be expected. After all, remember that every experience that you have is an experience of some THING, some object of perception. Pure Awareness is so simple (because there is no-thing there) and our lives are so focused in an outward direction that we tend to not know or remember that this silent Pure Awareness is the essence of what we are. Pure Awareness seems therefore very abstract and so unlike our other experiences that it is common when you first experience it to not be sure that you did. After all, our only database of experiences prior to a few moments ago was of the experience of things. So if you aren't sure if you experienced it, go back and go through the exercise again. Remember that you are not trying to experience something that's an object. It's just the silent witness of your experience, just your awareness itself, that with which you experience everything else.

Now that you have directly experienced Pure Awareness you may see what I mean by how simple and easy it is to have this experience. This is because there is nowhere to go, there is nothing to do. It is just a matter of noticing the background of silence in which your thoughts and perceptions are occurring. That's it. It is simply your own awareness being aware of itself!

This is a unique experience because all of our other experiences are characterized by our awareness experiencing things, objects of experience, like this book and the words printed on the pages, the feeling of the paper and binding that you are touching with your hands, the sounds that the pages make as you turn them, the taste of the food that you had at your last meal or snack.

All of the sensory experiences that we have are comprised of three components:

But the experience of Pure Awareness that you have just had is different. It is your awareness being aware of awareness itself. That means Awareness is Aware of Awareness. Awareness is not an object of experience. There is no perceiving going on. There is just a state of being Purely Aware. This is why we call it Pure Awareness because it isn't anything but Awareness experiencing itself.

Once you have done the exercise and experienced Pure Awareness you now have the experiential basis for understanding the rest of this book. Congratulations! You've already learned one of the Pure Awareness Techniques!

The Five Pure Awareness Techniques

You've already experienced the GAP Technique, which is number two on the list of the five pure awareness techniques. It is the simplest and most direct way to experience Pure Awareness that I know of. You can use it any time you want to reconnect with your essential self.

Why is the GAP Technique number two on the list of Pure Awareness Techniques when we have just started with it? Although it is the easiest one to for providing a very quick and simple way to directly experience Pure Awareness and therefore have a foundation of direct experience of Pure Awareness, it is the CORE Technique that has the position of number one in our list of the Five Pure Awareness Techniques. This is because the CORE Technique is the primary technique for removing the barriers to experiencing Pure Awareness all the time. It is also the one that is the most important for helping you to come out of the grip of emotional pain.

Different kinds of life circumstances require different kinds of tools to bring you back to the direct experience of Pure Awareness. The reason that we have five Pure Awareness Techniques is so that regardless of what is happening in any particular moment, you will have the appropriate tool available for that moment. If you were to put the book down and go about your daily life, after a while you would forget about Pure Awareness and the experience of it would again become something lost to the background of life. You would no longer be aware of it and your life, your decisions; your actions would again be coming mainly from your thinking and your conditioning and not from being established in the essential nature of what you really are.

With the Five Pure Awareness Techniques, the goal is to cultivate a state of being in which the experience of Pure Awareness is never lost, to live in a state of being in which Pure Awareness is never overshadowed by all the other experiences of life. When you have cultivated this state you attain a permanent state of inner peace that is undisturbed by even the most extreme circumstances. This is true liberation from suffering. This is true fulfillment of life. And, it typically develops quite rapidly from practicing these techniques.

Here's a top level summary of the Five Pure Awareness Techniques:

CORE—Center Of Remaining Energy

- Feeling into the Core of the Energy of the Feeling

- The technique for rapidly and thoroughly completing unresolved painful experiences without suffering

- This technique brings you back to the experience of Pure Awareness when you have become lost to the grip of emotion

- Because the CORE technique takes you into the core of the remaining energy of unresolved experiences and feelings it is an ideal acronym for this technique

GAP—Greater Awareness Place

- Experiencing Pure Awareness in the gap between thoughts or by noticing the background of silence in which the thoughts occur

- This is the technique for directly experiencing the essential nature of who and what you really are—Pure Awareness

- This technique brings you the experience of Pure Awareness any time you want to have it

- Because the GAP technique gives you the direct experience of the Greater Awareness Place it is an ideal acronym for this technique

AGAPE—Accessing the Greater Awareness Place Everywhere

- Experiencing Pure Awareness Everywhere

- The technique for directly experiencing that the essential nature of who and what you are is the same as the essential nature of everything in the universe

- This technique allows you to experience Pure Awareness everywhere and so it is very useful for reestablishing the experience of Pure Awareness when you are feeling isolated or separate from life and would like to ground yourself in a deep sense of connectedness with everything and everyone

- The word Agape is considered to be the Greek word for universal or unconditional love. That is exactly what is cultivated by doing this technique so it is an ideal acronym

WAIT—Waiting Accesses Intuitive Truth

- Wait for clarity and only make decisions from a stable state of Pure Awareness

- This is a technique for insuring that all of your decisions and actions are coming from a state of being in which you are stable and grounded in Pure Awareness

- This is the technique for being certain that your decisions are aligned with who and what you really are, that they are the expression of your "knowing" rather than your conditioning and thinking.

WONDER—Wait On Neutral During Extreme Reactions

- Unplugging the power cord/shifting to neutral on habitual and reactive thoughts and behaviors

- The technique for eliminating unwanted habits

- This technique helps you to cultivate the experience of remaining in Pure Awareness during extreme experiences and dismantle reactive habits

- It helps you to remain grounded in Pure Awareness even during extreme pleasure or pain

Now we'll go into each one of these simple, powerful techniques so that you can thoroughly learn how to do them and when to use them. If your experience is like the many thousands of others who have learned these techniques, you will experience them as some of the most precious, some of the most profound, and some of the most important tools that you will ever learn in your life.

CORE

Center Of Remaining Energy

Let's say your partner has just done something that really made you angry. You're very upset and now you feel like you just want to punch them out or scream at them or walk out on them. Or you've just heard some bad news and you are gripped by the feeling of sadness and disappointment. Or your partner has just done something that makes you feel hurt and resentful.

You are caught in the grip of an emotional reaction. Most people are NOT skilled at dealing with this kind of situation very well. They tend to take actions based on these kinds of emotional reactions that they later regret. It's pretty common, in fact it's widely accepted as just the way that life is. We also have lots of rationalizations and justifications for these behaviors and actions. But these excuses don't reduce the harm that comes to others, to our relationships and to our own happiness as a result of being the victims of our emotional reactions.

Would you like a way out? If so, I have news for you. The way out turns out to be... IN. Before I go too far in again trying to explain something that you haven't yet experienced, let's go to the web again and listen to some examples of me guiding people through the CORE Technique. Then I'll give you a step by step description of how to do it.

Here's the web page with the audio recordings of examples of the CORE Technique. Go listen to them now.

http://greatlifetechnologies.com/COREExercise.html

· · · · · ·

Welcome back.

Now that you've heard examples of people being guided through the CORE technique you can learn how to do it yourself. I recommend that you find a practice partner and go through the exercise with one of you guiding the other. Then switch roles so that you both get to guide each other as well as be guided by each other through the process. Practicing the CORE Technique with someone guiding you through the first few times usually makes it easier to learn than by simply doing it yourself.

In order to learn it, you have to be able to find the sensation of any unresolved emotion that is held in your body. We all know what it feels like to be angry or afraid or sad. With anger there is a raging energy that courses through us. We may feel it in our throat or our chest or our belly or it could be anywhere. With sadness or fear it is often in our chest but again it can be anywhere.

Start with an emotional charge that is easy to get at. A recent upset, a disappointment, a resentment, something that pissed you off and you're still a bit upset (or really upset!) about it or something that you are dreading having to do, something you committed to do and now wish you hadn't. You could kick yourself for agreeing to do it. How about a former lover who you long for, or a co-worker or family member you just can't stand, or something you are apprehensive about doing, asking for a raise or asking that cute redhead down the hall out on a date. Find anything that has a residual charge to it, a feeling of discomfort and think about it for a moment.

If you can feel that there is still a charge to it and you can feel the charge somewhere in your body then this will work for learning this technique. You have to have something that you can feel in your body in order to learn this. If you can't feel anything then we'll do a little provoking of a feeling in just a minute. But for now, if you can identify the sensation of—or the energy of—an emotion in your body then we can start with that.

The CORE Technique

We tend to hold the patterns of incomplete experiences in our bodies. These incomplete experiences are made of energy and the field of this energy typically feels kind of like a hurricane. The intensity of the energy is stronger at the center and weaker at the edges.

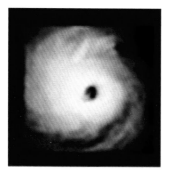

Allowing yourself to experience the core of the most intense part of the energy of an incomplete emotional experience is like sky diving right into the center of the eye of the hurricane. There is a stillness in the middle of it. It is actually safest and easiest to place your attention in the center of the most intense part of the energy of the feeling.

This technique is the most powerful, quick and effective way of resolving incomplete experiences I have found. When you put your awareness into the core of the most intense part of the energy of the incomplete experience, you allow yourself to complete the experience efficiently. When you stay out at the edges or even avoid allowing yourself to experience the energy of the incomplete experience at all, you tend to hold onto it and it remains incomplete and becomes

We have a tendency to avoid the intensity of the energy of a feeling and take our awareness out towards the edges of the energy to avoid being overwhelmed by it.

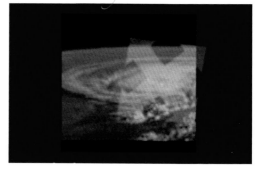

an invisible barrier to clear decision making and a barrier to being clear about anything, including even knowing what to do or who you really are.

Sometimes there are layers to an incomplete emotional experience, one stacked on top of the other. As you dive down into the core of the energy, it seems to be gone but then there is another layer of the incomplete experience there. Find the core of the new layer and dive down into it. Sometimes there can be several layers each with a different quality of feeling to them.

I had this experience the first time I did the CORE Technique. The first layer was anger. When I had felt into the core of the anger so thoroughly that there wasn't any anger left, I found a feeling of hurt under where the anger had been. Again I felt down into the energy of the feeling of hurt until there was nothing left to feel. Under that there was sadness and then a feeling of being alone and isolated. When I had felt into the most intense part of each of these layers of unresolved feelings I finally "came out the bottom" and there was nothing left at all. It was like the clouds burning off in the morning sun. Everything felt like it opened up and expanded and I was in a clear experience of Pure Awareness. So if there are layers of feelings stacked one on top of the other, just find the center of each one in turn and feel down into them until there is nothing left to feel.

Sometimes the layers of an incomplete emotional experience have been stored in several different places on your "internal hard drive" (your body). So you may find that when the energy of one of them seems to be fading away, the sensation of the presence of energy of another layer will start to be experienced in another part of your body. Whether there are several layers or just one, and whether the layers are in one location or in several, when you feel your way down into the core of the most intense part of the energy of the sensation you will eventually find... nothing.

The nothing that you will become aware of is the nothingness out of which you create all of your experiences, including the energy of your reaction to the negative experience that you have been holding there. Actually all that this energy is, is an incomplete experience. The energy that we are resolving with the CORE Technique is the remaining energy of your initial reaction, the experience of which was not completed at the time of the reaction. When you efficiently complete the experience of the reaction there is often a sense of the energy diminishing and then dissipating. This happens as you get back to the source of the energy from which the reaction was created in the first place. This source of the energy is Pure Awareness and you will recognize it as what you experienced when you did the GAP Technique for directly accessing Pure Awareness in the background of silence in which our thoughts occur.

This nothingness from which the energy of the reaction was created corresponds very well to the description of the Unified Field in quantum physics. It is postulated that when you complete the experience of the energy of the reaction that you have been storing, you are then directly experiencing the quantum field from which the energy of the experience had manifested.

Mastering this ability is a great skill that allows you to quickly come out of the limiting influence of the previously incomplete experience. It is the quickest way known to come out of the grip of an emotion.

How to Do the CORE Technique

Have your practice partner read the following instructions to you while you sit comfortably with your eyes closed. If you don't have a practice partner and/or you would like some professional help in learning the CORE Technique we have a large team of highly trained Core Dynamics Coaches who can guide you to do this over the phone or in person. You can visit the Great Life

Feeling into the Core
of the Most Intense Part
of the Energy of the Feeling

Coaching web site at www.greatlifecoaching,com and find a Core Dynamics Coach of your choice by reviewing their profiles. Receiving guidance in how to do the CORE Technique is easily done over the phone by these skilled coaches. So whether or not there is someone in your local area you won't need to meet in person to learn it. You can be guided in learning and doing the CORE Technique via a phone coaching session.

If you do have a practice partner, have them read the following instructions to you. Note that the text in italics is instructional for the person reading and is not meant to be read out loud.

After you have identified an issue that has a remaining emotional charge to it you are ready to start.

Reader—Read the sections in quotes " " out loud and read the bold sections silently to yourself—start here:

"Please close your eyes."

Wait for a few moments, then say -

"Notice that the sensation of the incomplete experience has an energy to it.

Wait for a few moments, then say -

"If you allow yourself to, you will notice that you can experience this energy somewhere in your body

pause

in your throat, chest, solar plexus, gut... somewhere.

Wait for a few moments, then say -

Where in your body do you feel the sensation of the energy of this incomplete experience?"

They will say or gesture to an area in the chest or stomach or throat or somewhere. Then say -

"If you allow yourself to, you can sense in that field of energy that there is an area where it is more intense than it is elsewhere. Can you sense that?"

They will typically acknowledge this with a nod or a yes. If not you can tell them to just allow themselves to feel the field of the energy for a little while and see if after a time they notice that there is an area that is more intense than elsewhere. In a short time they will tend to say yes. If not, you may have to use the guidelines for one of the variations of the CORE Technique that are explained later in this chapter. Assuming that they do acknowledge sensing an area in the field of the energy that is more intense than say:

"Now allow yourself to let your awareness go right into the center of the most intense part of the energy of the sensation.

pause

Can you do that?

Pause – (get acknowledgment)

Okay, go ahead and continue."

Now... WAIT, until you have a sense that it's appropriate to speak again. This will range from less than a minute to a minute or two or even more. Then say -

"Usually what happens is one of three things. Sometimes the sensation will become more intense at first as you haven't been allowing yourself to feel it fully. Sometimes it will seem to stay the same for a time. And sometimes it may start to fade away or soften. Is one of these things happening?"

Typically they will nod or say yes. If they don't volunteer anything you can ask –

Which one of these are you experiencing?

There are three possible responses :
1. It's getting more intense
2. It seems to be staying the same or
3. It seems to be fading away or becoming softer/less intense

For either 1 or 2 you can then say –

"OK, simply continue to allow your awareness to feel right into the center of the most intense part of the energy of the sensation."

Then give them some time to do that.

For #3, they say that it is fading away/becoming softer or less intense, then say -

"Bring your awareness in closer to whatever is left of the sensation, again find the center of intensity of the remaining energy, and again allow yourself to feel down into it, just experiencing the essence of the energy."

"The idea is to feel down into the energy of the sensation so thoroughly that there is nothing left to feel."

Then give them some time to do this. Then check in again with them to see what is happening. You can say –

"How's it going?"

They may have had some visual experience or the energy they are sensing may have moved to a different place or they may have completed the experience and the energy will have dissipated, and there's nothing left. If they say anything other than that what they found in there was nothing, you have to continue to guide them into the core of the energy of the experience some more.

"Is there any of the sensation of the energy left" or "Is there any charge left?"

If they say yes, then say -

"Okay, I'd like you to again place your awareness into the center of the most intense part of whatever is left of that energy. We're not looking for insights, just experiencing the energy of an incomplete experience. This is just the process of completing the experience of the energy that has been held in your body. I'd like you to allow yourself to experience it so thoroughly that there is nothing left to experience."

Continue with them in this way, in the vast majority of cases, the person will come out of the grip of the energy of the incomplete experience, and they'll say something like, "It's better" or "It's gone" or "there's nothing there."

Once they experience that there is nothing left and there is no more energy of the sensation you can now do what is called a provocation test. This is to make sure that they really fully experienced every bit of the energy of the incomplete emotional experience and there's truly nothing left of it. Say to them –

Now that it appears to be gone we are going to check to see that its really complete. So I'd like you to think about the original thing that was causing this sensation in you.

Give them a moment. Then say -

Is there any charge still associated with the original experience? Is there any remaining charge to the feeling that was originally there?

Typically, they'll say "No. It's gone." (Don't be surprised if they smile or look relieved.) Then you can say this –

"You are no longer limited by the presence of the energy of that incomplete emotional experience. Your body has been trying to get you to fully feel this energy and complete the experience that was held there. Now it is complete and your body has stopped creating this energy. There was an experience of something there that your body needed you to get, not intellectually but experientially. From this place that you're in now, this place of nothingness, you have total freedom of choice...you're in a state of all possibilities."

They may have opened their eyes by now but if they haven't you can invite them to do that now. This is the end of the guidelines for doing the CORE Technique.

You can continue reading the book by yourself now.

When to use the CORE Technique

So that is how you do the CORE Technique. You can use this any time you feel like you are getting lost to the grip of an emotion. Sometimes a circumstance will trigger some incomplete experience from the past and you will feel an emotional charge. This is a perfect time to remember to use the CORE technique. Once you come out of the grip of the emotion, you are now in a state of Pure Awareness. You can make the best decisions for your life from this state—but not when you are in the grip of emotion. Use the CORE Technique every time you feel that your emotional reactions are getting the best of you and you will never have to be the victim of your emotions again.

You can use the CORE Technique in two different ways.

1. Use it to come out of the grip of emotion whenever you feel you are becoming overwhelmed or just have some feeling that you would like to resolve.

2. You can use the CORE Technique in the context of Core Dynamics Coaching sessions. A trained Core Dynamics Coach will ask you questions to help you identify any "archived" incomplete emotional energy that may be causing a barrier to you having the life you want without your realizing that you are holding onto something. In this case the Core Dynamics Coach skillfully inquires into the nature of what is happening and is able to gently get you in touch with anything that might be blocking you from operating from Pure Awareness. They will then carefully guide you through the use of the CORE Technique (or the other Pure Awareness Techniques as appropriate) to resolve the basis of your inner conflict and remove this self-sabotaging inner barrier from your life.

In both cases the CORE Technique is the same. You feel down into the center of the intensity of the energy of the feeling until you have felt it so completely that there is nothing left to feel.

A few words of additional guidance here may be helpful. Because we are deeply conditioned to want to go away from where the emotional energy is the most intense, we will have an automatic tendency to not use the CORE Technique. It takes going through the process so many times, that we have developed a new habit of using the CORE Technique instead of avoiding and archiving our emotionally intense experiences.

This leads us to the next important point –

The Biggest Mistake You Can Make

The biggest mistake you can make with the CORE Technique is also caused by our early childhood conditioning. Sometimes, especially when people are first learning how to do the CORE Technique, they will feel into the feeling for a while and it will become less. Instead of completing the experience they will open their eyes and say, "It's better." The biggest mistake you can make with the CORE Technique is to NOT complete the experience of the energy that is being held there in your body. It is our conditioning—the Core Dynamic of Resisting Feeling Things Fully that causes us to want to go away from where the feeling is intense. You feel like you want to stop and not feel it any more under these circumstances. Therefore, it is very important to understand this dynamic and to keep feeling down into the center of the intensity of the sensation until there is nothing left to feel. These are the important words to remember –

"Feel into the core of the energy of the feeling so thoroughly that there is nothing left to feel."

Doing the MapQuest Thing

Something that can help to insure that you do feel into the core of the energy until there is nothing left to feel is to do what we call the MapQuest thing. Everyone who uses the internet knows about MapQuest. There are other similar mapping programs, however this was one of the first mapping web sites so it gives a familiar name to this idea.

When you are using MapQuest and you want to get a closer view, you "click in" meaning that you click the map and there is a "zooming-in" effect that lets you see a greater level of detail. It is like increasing the magnification using a telescope or a telephoto lens from an airplane or satellite.

 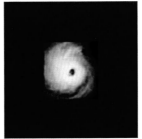 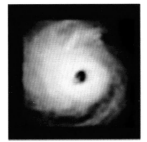

When you are feeling into the core of a feeling and it starts to fade away, rather than succumbing to the tendency to call it a day and stop feeling into it, "click in closer" and bring your awareness in closer to whatever remains of the energy of the sensation in the body. Again, find the center of the remaining energy and continue to feel down into it. The idea is to keep clicking in closer and feeling into the core and clicking in closer and feeling into the core until there is nothing left to feel.

A related issue is the attitude that you hold regarding the emotions that are held in your body. Due to the conditioning of Resisting Feeling Things Fully, we can have a tendency to have adopted an attitude of wanting to "make the bad feeling go away!" This is because of our fear of being overwhelmed by the feeling. We have a lifetime of perpetuating the childhood notion that we can't handle the feeling and are going to be overwhelmed by it. This can cause us to try to force the completion of the experience of the energy of the feeling when doing the CORE Technique. However this is counter productive. Forcing it will tend to cause straining and resistance and actually can get in the way of you allowing yourself to fully complete the experience. So just know that doing the CORE Technique is not about "making the feeling go away" or "getting rid of the feeling." Instead have the idea that you are gaining the skill of completing incomplete experiences. It is the completion—of the experience—of the energy—of the feeling in the body that allows the body to be able to stop creating that energy.

The body creating the energy of emotions is something quite natural to us, and key to our survival. If we are standing on the railroad tracks and a train is coming toward us, thank goodness our body has the innate intelligence to create the emotion of fear and motivate us to get off of the tracks. The same applies to walking up to the edge of a cliff. The fear that is generated in the body keeps us from going over the edge.

What this means is that when there is an incomplete emotional energy stored in the body, then there is some experience that our body is trying to get us to complete. The attitude of "getting rid of it" tends to cause us to stuff or repress the feeling. This is ignoring the body's innate intelligence which is trying to bring us some kind of experiential wisdom through completing the experience of the sensation that the body is creating. Therefore, it is important to shift your attitude from one of "making it go away" to "allowing yourself to complete the experience."

Laser Beam versus Flashlight Beam

Yet another related experience that can happen during the CORE Technique is that sometimes it may seem like it is taking a long time to complete the experience of the energy of the sensation or feeling. If this happens it may be an expression of some of the subtle influences of the Core Dynamic of Resisting Feeling Things Fully. Due to the tendency and habit of going away from where the energy of the sensation is the most intense, your awareness may tend to "spread out" and be more like a flashlight beam— rather than focused like a Laser beam. If your awareness is more like a flashlight beam then you won't tend to complete the experience of the energy of the feeling very quickly. Although we aren't in a rush when we're doing the CORE Technique, we do want to be efficient about completing the experience. This is why we go to the center of the intensity of the energy of the feeling. This is where we get to experience the real essence of the feeling, the most concentrated part of its energy. This allows us to complete the experience in the most efficient possible way.

When we use a laser like focus of our awareness when doing the CORE Technique, it can make the difference between it taking just moments versus taking hours or days to complete the experience. You will find that you become more effective with practice. Each time you do the technique you'll get better and better at it. After doing the CORE Technique a couple of dozen times, you'll discover that many times you will feel down into the energy of the feelings in a laser like way and they will be completed literally in seconds. Decide to become a "black belt" master of using the CORE Technique. Developing this mastery will serve you very well throughout your entire life.

Subtle Variations of the CORE Technique

Now I'll tell you about some of the different kinds of things that you may experience and give you some refinements and subtleties of the technique.

There is a wide range of possible experiences using the CORE Technique and as you do it more and more you may experience many of these. It may be useful to know the lay of land of your inner landscape of stored emotional energies just so that you will not resist your natural experiences or be concerned about any of these things that may show up.

The Eye of the Hurricane

As explained earlier, sometimes as you feel down into the energy of the sensation or feeling in the body, it will seem as if there is a vortex, a kind of eye of a hurricane right in the center of the energy. If your experience is like this, let your awareness be like a laser beam going right down the center of the vortex. Keep following it down until you "come out the bottom" and it will open up into the experience of Pure Awareness.

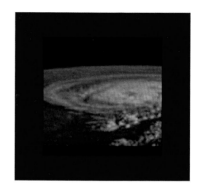

What if I feel like crying?

Sometimes you may feel like the energy is just too intense and you may feel inclined to be sucked into it or overwhelmed by it. You may feel like you are about to cry. There's nothing wrong with crying but it may not be the most efficient way to completely resolve the energy of the incomplete emotion that is held there. If you think about it for a moment, at what age did you learn to be overwhelmed by emotions and collapse into the overwhelming feeling and cry? Pretty young, that's for sure! Allowing ourselves to collapse into crying and be overwhelmed by the energy of an emotion is a learned behavior from a time when your capacity to feel things was much less than it is now. You were very young and had a delicate nervous system that was easily overwhelmed. You may have developed the habit of crying at that time because it was all you could do.

Certainly there is some release from the emotion that happens from crying but often there will still be residual energy there that can be triggered again by certain circumstances. Crying then becomes yet another way to avoid feeling into the core of the energy. Our aim is to resolve these incomplete experiences that are being held in the body so thoroughly and completely that they no longer are a barrier to our experiencing Pure Awareness all the time. As long as we continue to avoid feeling these incomplete feelings held in the body, they act as a kind of screen in between us and the continuous experience of Pure Awareness.

Therefore, you may find it more helpful to take your awareness inward to the center of the intensity of the incomplete emotional energy and feel down into it until the experience is totally complete. This will free you from any residual energy that the body is trying to get you to feel. The body is very tenacious. It will keep producing the same energy until you allow yourself to complete that experience. Once it is complete then you are free of it forever.

It's like running anti-virus software on yourself. Once the virus is gone, it's gone and won't come back again unless you have another traumatic experience similar to the previous one that put it there. But there is very little likelihood of this happening because you are much bigger and stronger now—particularly now that you know how to do the CORE Technique. The CORE Technique will help you avoid having the energy that you have already completed ever coming back... for two reasons.

1. As you do the CORE Technique more and more, you will become increasingly able to stay present to intense experiences without being overwhelmed. Your experience will be that you can stay present to emotional intensity much more easily because you have been exercising your "feeling" capacity. When you fully experience things as they happen, your body doesn't have to "archive" the incomplete emotional energy and store it for later processing.

2. Even if you do have another overwhelming experience that is similar to the one that you completed using the CORE Technique before, you have the CORE Technique which you can simply use to complete any new or similar incompletion that you may have in the moment. No problem.

Patterns of Energy that You May Not Recognize at First

Sometimes when there is something to feel into it may not at first be obvious that what you are feeling is a pattern of energy. This is especially true for things like feeling "empty" for example. Emptiness doesn't seem like it would be a feeling or a pattern of energy. So the trick to being able to catch these patterns of energy that don't even seem like they could possibly be patterns of energy and certainly don't seem like "feelings" is to use the very nature of what they do "feel" like as the way to get at them.

In other words, if you are feeling empty, you allow your awareness to go to the area that feels the MOST empty. This is a version of the most intense part of the energy of the feeling. There is a subtle but important difference between the "feeling of emptiness" and the experience of Pure Awareness. The feeling of emptiness has implied in it that there is an expectation that something should be there. There is a feeling that there should be something there and something is missing. Whereas, in Pure Awareness, even though there is nothing there to experience in the form of an object of experience, the sense of "no-thingness" feels alive. It feels vibrant and alive and there is a sense of limitless potential, a feeling of pure possibility. Pure Awareness is the source of all of our experiences. Emptiness is the experience of feeling the lack of something. In Pure Awareness there is no sense of lack.

So if you feel "empty" then feel into the most intense part of the emptiness. This brings up another important point about the CORE Technique. There may be a tendency to begin to think that the feelings that come up and the experience of feeling into them is going to be the same as it was each time that you have done it before. Although sometimes it may be similar, sometimes the quality of the experience of the energy will be different, in fact quite different as in the case of the "feeling" of emptiness.

There may be other feelings that surprise you because you would not characterize them as feelings. So it may be good to simply think of them as any experience other than Pure Awareness. Once you have done the CORE Technique and the GAP Technique many times, you are going to start to be quite familiar with Pure Awareness. You'll be able to tell when something you are experiencing is NOT Pure Awareness. If its bothering you, if it is making you uncomfortable, and especially if you don't want to feel it, that's the perfect indication that it needs to be felt and completed.

Using the Core Technique to Resolve the Incompletions that Cause Worry, Anxiety Nervousness and Depression

Another subtle variation of the CORE Technique is using it to resolve the underlying incompletions that cause Worry, Anxiety, Nervousness, and Depression. This is a wonderful application of the CORE Technique and you can use it right away to dissolve any of these feelings regardless of how long you have had them.

The reality is that what we call nervousness, worry and anxiety are actually just the outer edges of the energy pattern of fear. Here's the practical variation of the CORE Technique for resolving the underlying fear that is generating the nervousness, worry or anxiety.

Is there anything that you are worried, nervous or anxious about? If you think about it can you feel the energy of the worried or nervous or anxious feeling in your body? These kinds of feelings tend to either be everywhere or they may have the feeling of surrounding our body and enveloping it. What is actually happening is due to the conditioning of Resisting Feeling Things Fully. We have developed a habit of taking our awareness out to the outer edges of a feeling of fear so that we don't get overwhelmed by the fear itself. This experience of being out at the outer edges of the fear is what we call by these other names of nervous, worried or anxious.

So here's what you do. Allow yourself to feel the entire feeling of the field of the energy that comprises the worry, nervousness or anxiety. Just allow yourself to be fully present and feel the whole of its energy. What will gradually happen is that you will start to notice that in the field of energy, there is an area where it is more concentrated, more condensed. It will usually tend to be toward the center of the body somewhere, in your chest or solar plexus or belly (but it could be anywhere). Once you notice it you can now use the CORE Technique to allow your awareness to penetrate right down into the center of the most intense part of the energy of the feeling. You can continue using the rest of the CORE Technique in the normal way—making sure that you click in closer and feel into the Core of the energy of the feeling until there is nothing left to feel.

When it is all complete and there is nothing left to feel, open your eyes and immediately think about the thing that was worrying you or making you feel nervous or anxious. Do you still feel that way? I'll bet not. If you do, go back and complete the experience of whatever is left of that feeling.

The same thing applies for depression. Depression is simply the outer edges of sadness. It may be a very painful sadness, so we are again habituated to going out to the outer edges of the sensation of the sadness in our body.

The technique is the same as for worry and anxiety. Start by allowing yourself to feel the entire field of the energy of the depression. You will gradually start to notice that there is a more condensed or concentrated area within the field of the energy of the depression. You will typically find it more towards the center of the body.

Once you are aware of the more condensed part of the field of the energy of the depression, allow your awareness to penetrate down into the center of the most intense part of the energy of the sensation. Using the CORE Technique, click in closer and closer and keep feeling into the center of the most intense part of the energy of the feeling until there is nothing left to feel. Scan the whole area inside of your body where the sadness energy was being held. Make sure that you have felt it so thoroughly that there is nothing left to feel.

Now see if you can provoke it and feel the depression. Try to recall the feeling of depression and see what happens. You will be amazed that it is simply gone.

Underutilization of Our Innate Capacity to Feel

There is a reason that we have learned to avoid going where the energy of the feeling is the most intense. We learned it when we were very young. We all had emotionally overwhelming experiences when we were young, typically when

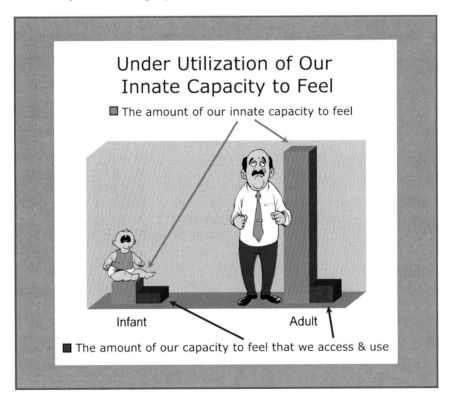

we were still pre-verbal. And we made a "feeling level decision" to try to not feel things so much in an attempt to not get overwhelmed by emotions. We really hate that when it happens so it's no wonder we make such a decision.

This decision seems to be quite universal. This "feeling level decision" does not have words to it, and this causes us to "Resist Feeling Things Fully." Resisting Feeling Things Fully is one of 12 Core Dynamics of Common Problems.

The Core Dynamics are a set of penetrating insights into the nature of pre-verbal human conditioning. I discovered them over many years of inquiry and research while developing the new field of Human Software Engineering™. It is this research that has also lead to the discovery and development of the Five Pure Awareness Techniques.

The Core Dynamics of Common Problems are organized into a model that shows their inter-relationships on an expanded Venn diagram that looks like this –

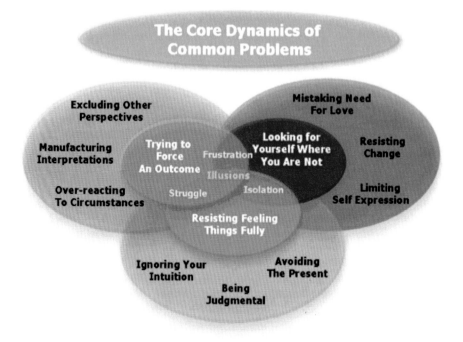

Each Core Dynamic is the expression of a "feeling-level decision" that we made when we were very young. These decisions were not made with words. They are pre-verbal and pre-cognitive. When we grow up and acquire verbal and cognitive skills, we forget that we made these powerful feeling-level decisions, such as the decision to do our best to avoid being emotionally overwhelmed by shutting down our access to our own innate capacity to feel. The in depth explanation is a topic for another book so we won't go into all of the details of the Core Dynamics here.

A more detailed understanding of the Core Dynamics is available via an audio CD set recording of my seminar on The 12 Core Dynamics of Common Problems. It is available via the web at –

http://greatlifetechnologies.com/CoreDynamicsCDSet.html

Scientific Research on Emotions and the Brain

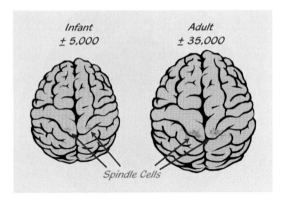

Infant
± 5,000

Adult
± 35,000

Spindle Cells

New brain scanning devices have allowed scientists to discover that certain cells in the brain are responsible for processing emotional experiences. Experiments were conducted whereby emotional stimuli were given to subjects while in the scanners to see which cells were activated. These brain cells are called spindle cells. The scanners showed increased blood flow to these cells during the emotional stimuli. These recent findings have now made brain researchers quite confident that spindle cells are involved with the processing of emotional information[1].

In addition, it was discovered that there are relatively few spindle cells in our brain during infancy. Thus, we really don't have a great deal of capacity to feel and process our emotions – we don't have the "physical hardware" to do it when are very young. Between infancy and adulthood there is apparently about a seven fold increase in the number of spindle cells in the brain – and thus a substantial increase in our capacity to experience a wider range of emotions. So, essentially as we grow, our bodies and brains acquire more and more "hardware" for processing feelings. However, due to our conditioning of Resisting Feeling Things Fully, this increased capacity tends to be grossly under utilized.

As a result of this under utilization of our innate capacity to feel things fully, we tend to not complete intense emotional experiences. This tends to cause us to accumulate "emotional baggage." We walk around with suitcases filled with these old unresolved, painful, intense feelings still held— seething inside of us. Whenever life settles down for a few moments, there they are: pressing up to the surface, wanting to be felt and healed.

Unresolved emotional pain

---

1   Humanity? Maybe It's in the Wiring, by **Sandra Blakeslee**, *New York Times*, December 9, 2003,

We tend to be resigned to this state, and assume that this is just how it is. It would be natural to make this interpretation due to the universal belief of everyone having very limited abilities to feel things. But surprisingly enough, this is not actually true. *It feels as if it's true… it's hard to believe it could be otherwise, but it's not true.*

Remarkably, as we mature, we acquire the spindle cells necessary to process our emotions… even the painful ones. But we are running on a three-year-old's decision to avoid feeling things fully so, we don't access and utilize the natural innate capacities for feeling that we already have. We do have "the hardware" to access the full spectrum of emotions that we were inherently designed to experience, but our software for accessing and using this hardware is disabled. We have a "bug" in our inner human software that is disabling our access to our own natural capacity to feel. We put a lid on it back when things just seemed to be too much to handle. This is why it can feel terrifying to even think about approaching that mountain of unresolved feelings… yet it can be easily done, without the fear of reliving awful experiences or having to fear that we will again be overwhelmed by them. Now it is possible to be free of them completely.

How E-motions (a.k.a. Energies in Motion) Are Created

The field of Quantum Mechanics has shed some fascinating light on the nature of existence... and our roles as creators.

It is of course now common knowledge that all matter is made out of molecules. These molecules are in turn made of atoms which are in turn made of subatomic particles. Physics now tells us that the subatomic particles are made up of waves of energy. All the tangible physical things you can see and touch in your world (i.e. cars, coffee cups, cell phones), plus the intangible things you experience (sounds, smells, tastes) are made out of waves of energy. In addition, all the things that seem even less tangible (thoughts, feelings, intuitions, perceptions, etc.) are also made of waves of energy. What distinguishes whether that energy manifests as a coffee cup, a dog barking, or a stressful reaction to an event appears to be the frequency patterns of the waves of energy, and their density.

There are countless studies documenting the electromagnetic properties of human beings. Our bodies, thoughts and feelings collectively create a unique electromagnetic human biofield that emanates from us. Recounting this research is not necessary here as this has already been brilliantly done by other authors including an excellent compilation by Dawson Church in his recent book, *The Genie in Your Genes*[2]. In addition technologies such as Electroencephalographs (EEGs) can measure our brain energy waves. Electrocardiographs measure the energy patterns of our heart, etc.

---

2   *The Genie in Your Genes, Epigenetic Medicine and the New Biology of Intention* - by Dawson Church

How does the energy of unresolved painful emotions impact us, as energy beings and in our daily lives?

One of Quantum Mechanics foundational principles is that everything is produced out of a field of pure potentiality, a limitless field of pure energy and information which has not yet become expressed in any physical form. The theory is that everything is created from this field of pure potential. This includes the experiences of our emotions. Our brain and body create the experience of emotion as a response to some outer stimulus. However, the emotion itself is a pattern of energy that we create within ourselves as an automatic reaction to a particular situation which is either pleasant or threatening. We use the term pattern of energy because different emotions have different vibrational patterns to them[3, 4]. This is how we distinguish between fear, anger, sadness, joy, ecstasy, etc.

When we have an experience that poses the potential for us to be harmed, we may respond with a "fight, flight or freeze" response. These responses are natural to all living creatures. We all have basic survival instincts built into us. Even flies don't want to be swatted and fly away if they can. When this occurs, a feeling gets produced inside our bodies. What we call an emotion is a sensation that we experience of a pattern of energy being created inside of our body.

---

3   Institute of HeartMath, a non-profit research organization that investigates emotional energy and intuitive development
4   Power vs. Force: The Hidden Determinants of Human Behavior, by David R. Hawkins, MD, PhD

Is This a Form of Therapy?

I have been asked if the CORE Technique is a form of therapy. My response to this is that although it may have a wonderfully therapeutic effect, i.e. it can relieve deep seated traumas and emotional pain, it is actually just a training in how to access and effectively utilize our previously underutilized capacity to feel. Everyone has this innate capability; we just haven't learned to use it.

This is similar to the development of the ability to read written words silently and understand their meaning. The ability to read written words that are formed out of combinations of individual letters is commonly attributed to the ancient Greeks, apparently something that developed about 2,500 years ago. This was a major advancement and simplification over the former Egyptian method of using hieroglyphics or pictures to represent spoken words. It made it much easier for people to learn how to read. However, initially all reading was done by speaking the sounds of the letters and words out loud. For centuries most people had to read out loud in order to understand the meaning of words and sentences. The ability to read silently was unusual for most people and only became widely taught and practiced in the 20th century. To quote Robert Wilson, a historian on the teaching of reading:

"Oral reading was usual. St. Augustine, for instance, was perplexed by St. Ambrose's habit of silent reading (in Confessions). The importance placed on it can still be seen by observing the lip movement of some religious people when they are reading their scriptures. It was only after the invention of the printing press made mass production of books possible, that silent reading became usual, but the recognition and teaching of it as a special skill had to wait until the 20th century."[5]

5   Used by permission from an article entitled *Teaching Reading—A History* by Robert McCole Wilson found on the internet at http://www. zona-pellucida.com/wilson10.html#r3. Author's address: Robert McCole Wilson, (87 Cottonwood St.) Box 838, Lake Cowichan, B.C., V0R 2G0

Imagine the amazement of the people who could read out loud but not silently when someone started to be able to read words and know their meaning without speaking them out loud. It might have seemed to be a miracle! And yet, now we take silent reading for granted. Human being's have had the capability to read silently all along but didn't always appreciate that they had it or know how to utilize this natural capability.

We all have the innate capability to feel things fully and to do the CORE Technique. We seem to live at a time in human development that is similar to the time when we only knew how to read out loud. Our ability to access and use our innate ability to feel seems to be quite limited by our conditioning.

The development of the CORE Technique is somewhat analogous to the invention of the printing press. Everyone can now learn how to do the CORE Technique and enjoy the enormous advantages of being able to resolve the unresolved emotional pain of the past and live more and more from Pure Awareness.

So is this a form of therapy? I think not. It is a form of training, a form of education on how to use formerly under utilized parts of our natural abilities. Anyone who can feel can learn to overcome their conditioning of being resistant to feeling, their conditioning of avoiding feeling and learn to use the CORE technique to clean up their inner emotional and energetic landscape.

Canada. Author's email: rmw@island.net

Remembering to Use the CORE Technique

The most important aspect of the CORE Technique is remembering to use it. Once you have learned it, it's a bit like upgrading your inner human software. Now you have a new icon of inner human software sitting on your desktop. Just like with computer software, this new capability isn't going to do you much good unless you double click on it and use it!

The best way to remember to use this wonderful new tool is to make a decision that you are going to become really good at it and that you are going to use it every time you get caught in the grip of an emotion. After you have done it a couple of dozen times you will have probably overcome the reticence about feeling your feelings so fully. Once this has been overcome the use of the CORE Technique will simply become a normal part of your skill set, like reading silently is. You won't have to try hard to remember to use it because it will have become a natural part of your life. It will be right there and you will use it whenever the need arises.

How Using the Core Technique Can Impact Your Life

There is a nice positive side effect of doing the CORE Technique many times. You will start to dismantle many of the life strategies of avoiding the possibility of being overwhelmed because you will gradually resolve your fears of that happening. This will allow you to start being more true to yourself, to start trusting and consistently act on your intuition, to become much less or completely non-judgmental and to be able to be fully present to just about anything. What all of these things have in common is that they require the ability to feel fully. Gaining mastery with the CORE Technique will allow you to find your life growing and becoming enriched in extraordinary ways that you never even knew were possible!

GAP

Greater Awareness Place

You have already experienced the GAP Technique at the very beginning of the book. That's how we made sure that you had a taste of Pure Awareness so that you could understand the rest of the book.

Now we'll go into the description of the GAP Technique in a bit more detail and also explain about when to use it, how to handle thoughts that come up during it, and special applications of the GAP Technique.

It would be a good time to take a few minutes and experience Pure Awareness again. Here's the URL for the recording of the GAP Technique.

http://greatlifetechnologies.com/GAP.html

Now that you have refreshed your experience of Pure Awareness by accessing it using the GAP Technique I'll give you a little bit more insight about the technique and how to get the most out of it.

How to Do the GAP Technique

You already know how to do that GAP Technique but there are some subtleties that may be helpful. First you have probably noticed that there are two ways to become aware of Pure Awareness during the GAP Technique. Both of them are more easily done with your eyes closed. In both cases it is good to start by allowing yourself to become aware of thoughts occurring in your mind.

For the first way, you simply notice that that there are gaps or pauses in between the thoughts. Sometimes it doesn't seem that there are any gaps when our mind is racing or when we are emotionally upset or disturbed. If this is the case, then what is needed is to shift to using the CORE Technique to complete the incomplete experience that is currently dominating your inner experience. Once you do this and it is complete then you will have a more settled state of being and be able to notice the gaps in between the thoughts.

The second way of accessing Pure Awareness through the GAP Technique is to notice that your thoughts are occurring in a background of silence. Normally we don't pay any attention to the background of silence in which the thoughts are occurring. Just as we don't pay attention to the silence in our living room when music is playing, we pay attention to the music. When we go to the movies we become absorbed in the images that are falling on the screen, so we don't pay attention to the blank white screen that allows the images to be seen. It gets overshadowed by the images. Similarly, the background of silence in which our thoughts occur is usually overshadowed by the "loudness" of our thoughts. Our thoughts are active, have meaning, sometimes have emotions associated with them and they are certainly more engaging when it comes to content than the background of silence in which they are occurring. So thoughts tend to attract our attention more than the silence does.

However, if we want to experience our essential nature which is our own Pure Awareness, it is a matter of simply "looking off to the side" of the thoughts and noticing that the thoughts are occurring in a background of silence.

Interestingly enough this can be done even when the mind is racing with lots of thoughts and there don't seem to be any gaps between them. This may be why some people prefer the "looking off to the side of the thoughts" approach over noticing the gaps, but either one will give you access to the experience of Pure Awareness. It's your preference but they are both really quite simple.

Thoughts, Thoughts and More Thoughts—What Do I Do?

Sometimes people become concerned that they are getting absorbed in thinking and that this seems to be getting in the way of the experience of Pure Awareness. They feel that thoughts are coming in and engaging their awareness again and again. It is important to have an understanding about the role of thoughts during the GAP Technique and to know how to handle them.

The answer is that there is nothing to handle. Having thoughts occur is not a barrier to experiencing Pure Awareness. It is perfectly possible to experience Pure Awareness and have thoughts occurring at the same time. It is a matter of what you favor noticing with your attention. It's certainly true that we are deeply habituated to noticing our thoughts. I would go so far as to say that just about everyone seems to be addicted to thinking. We do often use being absorbed in thinking as a "drug of choice" so that we don't allow ourselves to feel things.

But this doesn't mean having thoughts is a barrier to experiencing the background of silence even while thoughts are occurring. As you shift your attention from noticing thoughts to noticing the background of silence, allow yourself to really immerse your attention in that silent background. When you do this it is quite easy to simply allow yourself to shift your attention away from the thoughts and more toward noticing of the background of silence. Just as you can read a book with birds chirping outside or with the hum of traffic on the freeway across the way, you have the ability to direct your awareness to favor noticing one thing more than something else. It's just that we are so deeply conditioned to only notice our thoughts; we have not even known that there was a silent background in which the thoughts were occurring until now.

So as you do the GAP Technique notice that it is easy to allow yourself to favor noticing the silence of the background in which the thoughts are occurring. This silence is your own Pure Awareness. It is your consciousness. It is that aspect of you that allows you to experience all of life. This is why we refer to it as your essential nature. It is the silent witness or the observer of your experiences.

As you practice noticing Pure Awareness in the background of silence in which the thoughts occur, you may begin to have some extended periods of very clear experiences of Pure Awareness; sometimes there won't seem to be any thoughts at all. The thoughts may seem to fade so much into the background that you hardly notice them. When this happens it can be a very deep and satisfying experience. You will feel deeply refreshed and fully alive while also feeling deeply rested and relaxed.

As you practice the GAP Technique for longer periods of time, say 10 to 20 minutes, you may also have experiences of becoming absorbed in thinking for what seem to be long periods of many minutes. Sometimes when this happens people think that they are doing the GAP Technique incorrectly or that something is wrong with what they are doing. Nothing could be further from the truth.

When you become lost to thoughts during the GAP Technique this is actually because the technique is working beautifully!

What?

How could it be working if the idea is to experience the GAP and not the thoughts? There is a very special answer to this question that will allow you to take a whole new attitude towards the thoughts that occur while you are doing the GAP Technique. Here's what it is.

When you shift your attention to noticing the background of silence in which the thoughts are occurring, you are favoring noticing a state within you that is much less active than the active mind that is usually busy thinking thoughts. As you shift your attention to noticing Pure Awareness you will sometimes notice that you feel very relaxed. This is because you are naturally giving less energy to the mental activity of thinking. Therefore, your mind tends to settle down.

We tend to think of our body and our mind as separate things but really they are both parts of one wholeness of who we are. We experience less and less mental activity as we favor noticing the silent background of Pure Awareness. As our mind settles down it is natural for the body to settle down as well. This causes us to feel deeply relaxed. During this relaxation it is also natural for the body to begin to release any stresses or strains that may have accumulated. These may be minor versions of the incompletions that we have been describing during the explanation of the CORE Technique or other superficial stresses.

When stresses and strains begin to be released in the body this creates movement, activity in the body. This must create movement and activity in our mind because again the mind and body are so intimately connected. This means that when you become absorbed in thoughts while practicing the GAP Technique, it is actually a very positive by-product of the phenomenon of releasing stresses and strains. For that matter I've also had people fall asleep during the GAP Technique. This is the same thing. It's the body releasing some accumulated fatigue and so you fall asleep. It's all quite natural. When you do the GAP Technique if your body needs to release stress or fatigue it will take the opportunity to give itself what it needs. This is simply the natural functioning of the oneness of our mind and body.

Therefore, if you have lots of thoughts during a particular session of the GAP Technique it actually means that you have successfully accessed the GAP and settled the mind down even if it only took a very short time. It means that the body is releasing some stresses and strains. This in turn is creating the activity of thinking in a strong enough way that your mind becomes quite occupied with this activity. This is experienced as thoughts in the mind. It's not from doing it wrong. On the contrary, it is from doing the technique correctly!

So don't have the attitude that thoughts shouldn't be there. It's natural for them to be there. It is also natural for you to shift from noticing Pure Awareness to noticing the thoughts. Here's what you do about it.

When you notice that you have been absorbed in thinking, don't bother to chastise yourself. Actually, something good has just happened—you've released some stress. When the body has released enough stress that you become aware that you've been thinking, now it is time to go back into the GAP and experience Pure Awareness again. What there is to do at that moment when you become aware that you were thinking, is to gently shift your attention back to noticing the background of silence in which the thoughts are occurring.

Simply allow for the naturalness of both thinking and noticing Pure Awareness in the background of silence. There is a natural shifting back and forth between noticing Pure Awareness and being absorbed in thinking. The idea, after all, is to cultivate a clean inner landscape using the CORE Technique and to become completely familiar with Pure Awareness using the GAP Technique. Eventually you never lose the experience of Pure Awareness and it isn't overshadowed by thoughts or anything else. When you develop this state of being you experience Pure Awareness as present all the time, 24/7, 365—it never goes away. That's what we're after. When you reach this state (which can develop quite quickly with regularly using the Pure Awareness Techniques) not only will you be able to maintain the experience of Pure Awareness while you are having thoughts but even while having intense experiences of pleasure or pain. In this state you are never lost to your experiences and you experience a shift of the sense of who you are from being an individual to being Pure Awareness, which is the true reality of what you really are.

When to Use the GAP Technique

- As a regular daily practice to become very familiar with the experience of Pure Awareness

- Before doing something important to you where you would like to be operating from wholeness

- While working with a Core Dynamics Coach to experience that you are already whole and complete

- Any time you want to directly experience Pure Awareness

You can use the GAP Technique whenever you like, whenever you want to experience Pure Awareness. Some people like to make a regular practice of the GAP Technique and use it as a form of meditation that they do once or twice per day, typically in the morning and evening. The more you practice it the more you will cultivate an ever increasing presence of Pure Awareness. You can find the frequency and duration that suits your individual tastes and desires for developing your awareness of Pure Awareness. Making it a regular practice is highly recommended.

However, don't overdo it either. Sitting around doing the GAP Technique for hours at a time may not be the best plan for integrating the state of Pure Awareness into your life. What is optimal is to toggle back and forth between becoming familiar with Pure Awareness by doing the GAP Technique for short periods of time and then engaging in your daily activities. Balance is the key and introducing the GAP Technique into your daily routine starts you on a path of integrating Pure Awareness into your life experience. The value of doing this is enormous.

The GAP Technique is also very useful during Core Dynamics Coaching sessions whenever someone has become overly identified with things in their life. People tend to become identified and attached to their possessions, the people and relationships in their life, their thoughts and ideas, their emotions, reactions, stories and self-definitions. It is in the nature of human conditioning to become identified with both our inner and outer experiences and lose the sense of connection to our own essential nature—Pure Awareness.

During Core Dynamics Coaching sessions the Core Dynamics Coach will use the GAP technique to gently guide their client back to the experience of Pure Awareness when he/she identifies that the person needs to experience the inner reference of who they really are. It is a great experiential antidote when people have slipped into getting the sense of who they are from anything other than

Pure Awareness. This quickly re-establishes the inner sense of being grounded in one's Self. Many forms of attachment, struggle and suffering just melt away and are recognized for the illusions that they are and problems that they have caused. The GAP Exercise is a simple and fast way to bring someone out of all of the Core Dynamics in the categories that we call Looking for Yourself Where You Are Not and Trying to Force an Outcome.

For more about Core Dynamics Coaching or to find a Core Dynamics Coach go to - www.greatlifecoaching.com on the Internet. For information about Core Dynamics Coach Training programs please see www.greatlifetechnologies.com/CDCTraining/Options.html

Special Uses of the GAP Technique

My dear friend and colleague Michael Stratford who is the Director of the Core Dynamics Coach Training Program for Great Life Technologies came up with a wonderful use of the GAP Technique. It goes like this.

First go into Pure Awareness using the GAP Technique. Once you are clearly in Pure Awareness simply ask any important question you would like to have some guidance about and then wait and see what happens.

Typically you will get some kind of "knowing" or even very clear ideas that you may not have even considered before. You may get the guidance that there is nothing at all for you to do, or that there are very specific things for you to do to participate in bringing about that which you are inquiring about. This process is very similar to an ancient technique described by Yogi Patanjali, an Indian sage who is thought by some to be the father of the entire field of Yoga. He wrote about this process in a Vedic text called the Yoga Sutras.

Patanjali described a technique called sanyama in which you take your awareness to Pure Awareness and then drop a thought into Pure Awareness. The outcome of this practice is the development of something called Sidhis which translates as perfections. The idea is that when you have a thought at the level of Pure Awareness, it activates the support of the full power of the infinite potential of all of the laws of nature that are latent in Pure Awareness. This is a powerful way to bring yourself into alignment with these laws of nature. It is not commanding the laws of nature, it is learning how to be one with them, to bring yourself into alignment with them. Michael seems to have independently rediscovered some of Patanjali's insights. Experiment with it yourself after you have become more acquainted with experiencing Pure Awareness by using the GAP Technique.

Michael makes the analogy of dropping a question into Pure Awareness with the idea of putting a destination into a GPS system in a car. All of a sudden the path to where you want to go becomes totally clear.

Remembering to Use the GAP Technique

Remembering to use the GAP Technique is again dependent upon your desire and your decision about it. If you find that the experience of the GAP is useful to you and you like the lingering presence of Pure Awareness that develops as you do it more and more, then you may be inspired to practice the GAP Technique on a regular basis or as it suits you. Some people work well with routines and others don't but it will always come back to a decision. If you decide to use this technique to cultivate your familiarity with Pure Awareness then you will find the frequency and duration for doing the technique that suits your personal situation.

How Using the GAP Technique Can Impact Your Life

As you will notice, practicing the GAP Technique can give you a profound sense of inner peace, centeredness, relaxation and expansion of awareness. It can rapidly bring you the clear, direct experience of Pure Awareness. This tends to bring about a gradually increasing familiarity with Pure Awareness and more and more of a sense of awareness and presence in your daily life.

It can also be a way to shift how you get the sense of who you are from thinking of yourself as an isolated individual to experiencing yourself as the totality of Pure Awareness. It is therefore an extremely useful technique and worth practicing on a regular basis.

AGAPE

Accessing the Greater Awareness Place Everywhere

The AGAPE Pure Awareness Technique gives you the direct experience that the Pure Awareness you access via the GAP Technique is the very same Pure Awareness that is permeating everything in the entire Universe. This is not just an idea, or a mere intellectual understanding. It actually takes you through the direct experience of this.

How to Do the AGAPE Technique

It starts with the GAP Technique and then expands the experience of Pure Awareness from the sense of being localized in your head to your whole body, then to the room you are in, then the house or building that you are in, then the town or city, the country, the world, the solar system, the galaxy, the clusters of galaxies and the entire universe and beyond.

When you open your eyes after having this expansive experience of Pure Awareness you then allow yourself to feel the presence of Pure Awareness in an object that you can see and then in another person if you are in a place where there is someone else present.

The result is a sense of expansion of the experience of Pure Awareness that gives you the very real sense of your oneness with the entire universe and everything in it. It gives you the direct experience that what you are at your essence is the essence of every single thing that you could ever experience.

You can access the audio recording that guides you through the experience here–
http://www.greatlifetechnologies.com/AGAPE.html

If you don't have access to the Internet you can have a friend read the instructions to you. Here they are:

Experience Pure Awareness Everywhere

- This Pure Awareness Techniques is based on the ability to experience Pure Awareness through the GAP technique so in sharing this with others, it is first important to have them clearly experience Pure Awareness in the gap between thoughts or by noticing the background of silence in which thoughts occur.

- To start this technique, again ask the person to sit quietly and close their eyes, and to again become aware of the gap between the thoughts or the silent background in which the thoughts occur. Wait for about half a minute and let them renew their experience of pure awareness in the gap.

- Then say the following: "Notice that the sense of pure awareness may feel like it is inside of you, inside of your head. Notice that, if you allow yourself to, you can feel the lively presence of that pure awareness throughout your entire body." [Wait for about half a minute to allow them to experience this.]

- "Notice that, if you allow yourself to, you can feel the lively presence of that same pure awareness filling up the room that you are in now. It's already there. You are just allowing yourself to notice that it is there." [Wait about half a minute to allow them to experience this.]

- "If you allow yourself to, you can experience the lively presence of that pure awareness permeating the whole building, [pause for about 10 seconds], and it is permeating the whole city of _____ (name of city where they are)." [pause for another 10 seconds].

- "If you allow yourself to, you can feel the lively presence of that same pure awareness filling up the entire state of _____(fill in the name of the state where they are)." [Wait another 10 seconds].

- Continue in this same way with the country, the world, the solar system, galaxy, the clusters of galaxies, the whole unbounded universe.

- "Now bring your awareness back to your body and notice that you can do that without losing the sense of that expanded pure awareness that's permeating everything.

- "Now open your eyes when you are ready, and look at an object in the room. Notice that that same lively pure awareness is present there. In fact, it's present everywhere."

- "Now look at a person in the room (if there is one) an simply notice that the same lively pure awareness is there permeating that person. It's the same pure awareness that you experience inside of you when you notice the background of silence in which the thoughts occur."

- "Notice that pure awareness is permeating everything. It is the essential nature of what you are, it is the essential nature of what I am and it is the essential nature of everything that exists. That's all there is. It is all vibrating pure awareness. By practicing this exercise from time to time you can cultivate the awareness of Pure Awareness so that it is present all the time."

When to use AGAPE

- Directly following doing the GAP technique

- As a regular daily practice to directly experience that the essential nature of who and what you really are is everywhere in the universe

- Before doing something that is important to you where you would like to be operating from wholeness and experiencing yourself as One with everything and everyone

- Anytime that you want to experience being One with everything and everyone

Remembering to Use the AGAPE Technique

The guidelines for remembering to use it are fundamentally the same as for the GAP technique. Remembering to use the AGAPE Technique is again dependent upon your desire and your decision about it. If you enjoy the heightened and expanded presence of Pure Awareness that the experience of the AGAPE Technique brings you, then you may be inspired to practice it on a regular basis. Because it is a natural extension of the GAP Technique you can go from the GAP right into the AGAPE. If you decide to use this technique to cultivate your increasing familiarity with Pure Awareness then you will find the optimal schedule for doing it that suits your situation.

How Using the AGAPE Technique Can Impact Your Life

Often people feel isolated and alone, separate and disconnected from others and from life. The AGAPE Technique has a profound effect on bringing you out of the illusion of separateness and giving you a deep sense of connectedness with people, nature, the world and life as a whole.

WAIT

Waiting Accesses Intuitive Truth

The WAIT Technique goes against the grain of a lot of our societal conditioning. We are all conditioned to be impulsive and reactive. "Just do it!" When we are impulsive and reactive our decisions and actions are expressions of our learned conditioned responses. They are not expressions of Pure Awareness. There are times when it is essential to act quickly but this is distinct from being impulsive and most people are clueless that there even is such a distinction.

The vast majority of people live their lives as the product of their conditioning. They make decisions based on what they think they should do. They make decisions based on emotional reactions or moods. They make decisions and base their actions not on being true to themselves but based on responding to pressure or to some outer authority that they have learned to follow without even realizing that this is happening.

The result... misery, struggle, suffering.

Have you ever had the experience of having a desire and then forgetting about it only to have the fulfillment of the desire show up almost like magic without you having to do anything to bring it about? Pretty much everyone I've asked that question of has said yes. Isn't it great when that happens? How would you like to have your whole life have this kind of effortless alignment quality to it? Well, it's possible and the WAIT Technique is the key. Whether you have a role in making something happen or whether the universe and the laws of nature take care of the whole thing without you having to life a finger, the WAIT technique gives you the tool you need to align yourself with the principle of least effort. This is a natural principle that is operating at the basis of all of the amazing phenomena that the universe organizes seemingly without effort— because it is.

How to Do the WAIT Technique

In theory the WAIT Technique is pretty simple. You just... wait. But what do you wait for? And for how long? How do you know when you have waited long enough? The answer is that you wait for clarity. The trick is really getting what that means. What normally controls our decision making process? Typically we are motivated by our thoughts and our emotions. We aren't even making our own decisions. Our conditioned responses are deciding for us. We are programmed to react, not to decide.

In Human Software Engineering we distinguish between two kinds of thoughts (most people have no idea that there is such a distinction). These two kinds of thoughts are called natural intentions and conditioned responses.

By the term natural intentions I'm not talking about the "I'm intending this into reality" ego-based kind of meaning for intention. I mean the kind of intention like the desire you had that got effortlessly manifested without you having to lift a finger. Sometimes you are called upon to be involved but your involvement has the same quality of effortlessness as the kind of effortlessness that makes the grass grow or the clouds blow by. It's that "being totally in the zone kind of feeling", a sense of frictionless flow.

On the other hand, conditioned responses are learned behaviors. They are not effortless although we may have become quite competent at many of them. This may give them the appearance of being effortless, even though they are far from it. They tend to be more like trying to force things to be the way that we expect them to be, or trying to get other people to do things our way, or chasing after something because we are longing to get a sense of fulfillment from attaining it. All of the decisions and the ensuing actions are coming from thoughts that are generated out of stories about what we "think" should happen.

Everyone has the ability to KNOW what is right and correct for them but this is typically covered up by layers of conditioning and emotionally reactive habits. Think of impulsive purchases that you have made that you later regretted making. Getting into relationships that your intuition told you not to touch with a ten foot pole typically result in suffering. Making impulsive decisions about career or money or health issues can be disastrous.

The answer is very simple, but like all of the Pure Awareness Techniques it involves doing something that is the opposite of what we have been conditioned to do. That is to wait for clarity. Waiting for clarity means to not make decisions impulsively or emotionally. The basic guideline is: if your decision feels emotionally charged, don't make it, instead wait for clarity.

Waiting for clarity is not a passive process. Not at all. Waiting is a time to gather more information, let circumstances develop a little bit more, and especially it is a time to practice the other Pure Awareness Techniques. Use the CORE Technique for fully feeling any feelings that the potential decision is bringing up. And perhaps use the GPS version of the GAP Technique to check in with your Knowing and see what kind of guidance you get, even if all it says is, "not ready to give you an answer yet", which basically means... wait some more.

Like all of the Pure Awareness Techniques you have to actually do it, you have to experience it in order to start to get the hang of it. This one is a little different though as there isn't any audio file to listen to except one that you can choose to install inside of yourself that is a looped recording that says – Wait for clarity, Wait for clarity.

What does clarity look like? What does it feel like? It's not emotional. It's not pressured for time. It's not concerned about missing out on some opportunity. It is a calm inner quiet knowing that something is either right for you or its not. It doesn't have anything to do with what anyone else thinks or feels about it. This is called being true to yourself. What is it that you are really being true to? You are being true to your unique purpose in being here in this life. Waiting for clarity allows you the time to get to a place within yourself where you aren't reacting to outer demands. You are taking action based on a calm inner quiet knowing of what is right for you.

Many people have such a deep seated habit of acting on their impulses that they don't really know what waiting for clarity means. When you are clear about something the experience is definitely different than while you are still caught up in non-clarity. Non-clarity has a feeling of pressure about it, or a feeling of confusion or frustration or fear or a vague discomfort. These feelings may in fact be the vary barriers to having clarity in the first place. You can use the CORE Technique to feel into these feelings. Certainly completing the process of feeling into to core of the energy of a feeling brings you to a state of being in which you are no longer in the grip of the feeling. There's a quietness, a sense of expansion, a sense of wholeness.

It is from this place that clarity comes.

So when you experience clarity it will have a quality of calmness, peacefulness, settledness and a deep certainty that doesn't even need intellectual understanding. You simply know. This is the only real basis for making any kind of important decision about your life. The experience of what your KNOWING feels like may be different than the way someone else will experience it. What will be valuable for you is to cultivate your personal familiarity with what KNOWING feels like within you. There is no doubt there. There is no uncertainty or questioning things there. You simply know. This is what clarity is. This is what you wait for.

Each of us is here for a purpose. We all have our own rhythm and our own contributions to make according to how our individuality is designed (that's another interesting story for a different book[6]). If you are always impulsively responding to what you think you should do, or what will please someone else, or not doing things because you are afraid of some potential consequences that you don't think you can handle, you are going to be continuously experiencing frustration, anger, bitterness and disappointment.

So why not start to learn how to wait for clarity. It's so much better to align yourself with nature's principle of least action than it is to struggle to make things happen while living in a story that is disconnected with what is real. Allow yourself the pleasure of trying this out. The next time you are about to make an impulsive decision, wait before you make it instead and see what happens. You will be very, very glad that you did. And just a few times of seeing the magic that comes from waiting and you'll be a convert. You're gonna love it.

When to Use the WAIT Technique

- When someone is pressuring you to make a decision such as to buy something or make a commitment to do something

- Whenever you are making big decisions such as who to marry, where to live, what job to take, whether or not to start a new business

---

6   Living Your Design by Lynda Stone, coming soon at www.humandesigncommunity.com

- Anytime you have doubts

- While waiting, fully feel whatever there is to be experienced. Use the CORE Technique if needed.

Are We There Yet?

We get impatient when we have expectations that are not being met. The problem here is not what life is bringing us. It is that we are trying to dictate the timetable for the fulfillment of our desire to Life, the Universe, and the Laws of Nature. It's as if we are saying, OK God, Bring me the fulfillment of my desire on my timetable not yours!

Just the asking of the question, "How long do I have to wait?" is a clear indication that an expectation is in place. Clearly there is a disconnect between being present to the reality of the moment and attempting to have life show up the way that we expect it to rather than the way that it is.

We all know the experience of having the kids sitting in the back seat of the car asking over and over, "Are we there yet?" When you wait for clarity you don't have to ask anyone else what's happening. You are so present to the reality of the moment that you know what's happening. You don't have to ask someone else to make your decisions for you or tell you what to do because you aren't running on auto pilot or using some other authority to make decisions for you. You know when you are clear about something. You can also feel if you still are caught up in a wave of emotion about something and still need to wait longer. You have a certainty about your knowing that doesn't need to be explained. Or you have a certainty of knowing that it isn't time to know yet and you are completely OK with that.

Living in the Wonder of Uncertainty

We call this living in the wonder of uncertainty. Making the shift from living in the terror of uncertainty to living in the wonder of uncertainty is what we are after here. Most people are afraid of the unknown. This is what causes people to become "control freaks." We try to control things when we are afraid that something might happen that we can't handle, that something might cause us to become emotionally overwhelmed. This fear is the residue (or the residodo as my friend Barbara Dillinger would say!) of the Core Dynamic of Resisting Feeling Things Fully. It is the deeply engrained conditioned response that is controlling our choices and decisions about attempting to set things up so that they will be known and predictable.

Good luck! Things are not predicable or certain. Things are very uncertain. But uncertainty is only a problem if we are afraid that we won't be able to handle whatever shows up. What advantage could there possibly be in making decisions when you are not certain? What advantage could there be in basing your decision on anything other than having clarity? It doesn't make sense to be impulsive just because it is so habitual for the majority of the population to do that. After all, the thing that is driving this impulsive decision making is the terror of uncertainty. Do you really want that to be the basis of your decisions and actions? Of course not!

What if instead you used the CORE Technique and felt into the fear of uncertainty so thoroughly that you didn't have it anymore? What if you made a shift from living in the terror of uncertainty to living in the wonder and delight of uncertainty?

I remember clearly when this shift happened for me. Without realizing it I had been living in the fear of what might happen with a constant undercurrent of apprehension that something bad might occur. Something might happen that I wouldn't be able to handle. After practicing the CORE Technique for a few months I had the experience of this shift in my awareness. I shifted from having this constant undercurrent of fear about what might happen to a delightful kind of inner peace, a peace that had the certainty that whatever comes up, I'll be able to handle it.

People don't want to wait primarily because if they wait they will have to face their fears of uncertainty that intuitively they know will surface while waiting. So making the decision to wait for clarity is going cold turkey on your addiction to being impulsive. It is learning to stop using impulsivity as a means to escape your fears of uncertainty. Using the WAIT Technique is making a decision to start to be present to and begin to fully feel into and completely resolve your fears of uncertainty.

When you choose to wait for clarity before making decisions it is very important to realize that you will come face to face with your fears of uncertainty. It's very valuable to be conscious that this is going to happen. Fortunately, you already have the CORE Technique so you have the resources and the skills to face and handle the terror of uncertainty. You too can make a permanent shift from terror to wonder and delight.

It is so wonderful to begin to enjoy uncertainty instead of fearing it. While you still have fears of the unknown, the WAIT Technique will allow you to come face to face with them so that you can then use the CORE Technique to fully and completely liberate yourself from these insidious fears. It takes a decision and a commitment to yourself to pull this off. You now have the tools to be successful and you don't have to go it alone, by the way. If you want help making this shift, hire a Core Dynamics Coach to help you along the way. They have gone down this path themselves so they know the lay of the land. When you want to know how to get somewhere, ask someone who knows the territory to show you the way.

As with all of the Pure Awareness Techniques, you get better and better at doing the WAIT Technique with practice. But you have to start. One thing that you may not want to wait to do is to start waiting for clarity!

There is no set answer to the question of how long to wait. But the fundamental answer is to wait until you have that quiet, calm inner knowing that something is right for you or not. Different people experience this kind of inner knowing in different ways and you can only find the right way for you by waiting to see what it is. With practice you will know.

There is actually one other way to have insight about how you know things and how to make decisions that are correct for you and perfectly aligned with how you are designed to operate in this life. It's called Human Design. It is another new field that is highly synergistic with Human Software Engineering. Conveniently, my wonderful wife Lynda Stone just happens to be a leading expert in the world and one of the leading teachers of the Human Design System. In Human Design you can see exactly how you were designed to operate from the moment you were born. It is unlike astrology or any of the other esoteric systems like that. It provides you an individualized picture of where to look for your knowing, from where you will get your clarity. This is immensely useful and valuable. You can learn more about Human Design at Lynda's web site at www.humandesigncommunity.com.

Waiting allows you to begin to live in alignment with your own personal human design. It is what allows you to be able to live a strategy that is consistent with who you are designed to be and to be able to follow your inner guidance system instead of being driven by your conditioning and looking to others for the basis of your decisions and actions.

Why do we call waiting for clarity a Pure Awareness Technique? We want all of our decisions and actions to come from Pure Awareness. When we are caught up in our conditioned thinking, or expectations, or our emotional reactions, then we lose connection with Pure Awareness and our decisions have a faulty basis. Waiting allows us the time needed to reconnect with Pure Awareness by simply letting it show up. If we are practicing the other Pure Awareness Techniques it will show up as we go into the CORE of feelings that we have had triggered by the need to make this decision, or by going into the GAP and experiencing Pure Awareness. But even if we do these techniques we may not yet be in alignment with the universe's timing. Waiting allows us to come into that alignment so that we become part of the effortless mechanics of nature that are bringing about the fulfillment of our purpose. Waiting gives us the opportunity to live in the wonder of uncertainty. The wonder of uncertainty is Pure Awareness. That's why the WAIT Technique is a very important Pure Awareness Technique.

In a way, waiting for clarity is similar to the CORE technique in that we stay present to whatever is there whether it is the feelings inside of us, demands from outside of us or notions or expectations that just need to be reconsidered. The process of waiting for clarity is like the process of drilling down inside the core of a feeling until we get to Pure Awareness. In fact what clarity really means is having that same expansive, simple natural feeling that you get at the end of the CORE Technique or while you are experiencing Pure Awareness during GAP or AGAPE. You know when you are clear because clarity has that same inner knowing that needs no explanation. Then if there is anything for you to do it will be obvious and will have no charge to it.

Remembering to Use the WAIT Technique

This one can be a little tricky because we are so conditioned to be impulsive and reactive. You may not be making a clear distinction between spontaneity and impulsivity. Being clear about this distinction is an important key to being able to successfully use the Wait Technique. There are two simple rules for properly using the WAIT Technique. They are:

Rule #1 - When in doubt, WAIT

Rule #2 - If there is any emotional charge involved in the decision you haven't waited long enough yet (and you also need to use the CORE Technique!)

Waiting is truly a spiritual practice because so often the reason that you are not waiting is that if you did wait you would have to face some pretty uncomfortable feelings that would come up during the waiting. Some of us are addicted to our impulsivity even though it perpetually causes us suffering.

So again there is a decision to make. If you get it that waiting aligns you with the universal law of least effort and if you want to have your decisions and actions simply be part of the grand expression of the law of least effort, if you want to live in that perpetual "being in the zone" kind of place experience in which your desires are fulfilled with the least amount of effort, then I invite you to make a decision and a commitment to yourself that you will master the art of waiting for clarity. Try it. You'll like it!

How Using the WAIT Technique Impacts Your Life

Let's be realistic. At first waiting for clarity will push you up against all kinds of issues that you have been unwilling to face. But you do have the other Pure Awareness Techniques now to help you through those issues and feelings.

You will have to use the other techniques too. This is because one of the main things that happens while you are waiting is that feelings are going to come up. Facing and feeling these feelings will become the need of the moment when they show up. The process of waiting is what gives you access to these feelings. In fact it is often these very feelings that are the real barriers to clarity. Waiting without feeling fully is called impatience. Waiting with feeling fully is called patience. Waiting is not passive. It is one of the most powerful and dynamic choices you can make.

As you get the hang of it you will become a convert because you will begin to experience that lots of times the issue or problem just seems to resolve itself or go away. Having the experience of how much easier this makes your life can be inspiring to really adopt waiting for clarity as a strategy for your life.

As you get the hang of it you will become a convert because you will begin to experience how so much of the time the issue or problem just seems to resolve itself or go away. And if what you are waiting for is a job offer or a business opportunity, something magical happens while you are waiting for clarity about it. If it's the right decision for you, not only will it not go away, the offer will get even better during the waiting!

It's true and it happens all the time, but you have to have the courage to wait and see. That courage is actually the courage to feel the feelings that are going to come up in you while you are waiting. And now you have the tools to be able to do that with the CORE Technique.

Waiting for clarity, one of the greatest inventions since the wheel... of time.

WONDER

Wait On Neutral During Extreme Reactions

The WONDER Technique is also known as unplugging the power cord or shifting to neutral. These analogies capture the essence of this technique.

Imagine you are driving a car on a level road. You shift the car into neutral. What happens? You coast to a stop.

If you are using a vacuum cleaner and unplug the power cord while it's running, what happens, you hear the motor wind down and stop.

In both of these analogies the principle concept is that you stop feeding energy into the system. When there's no energy nothing happens.

If cultivating a state in which you live from Pure Awareness all the time is starting to sound appealing to you, then learning and practicing the WONDER Technique is going to be another great tool to help you be able to do just that. The primary barriers to enjoying the presence of Pure Awareness in our lives all of the time are our habitual conditioned responses and our incomplete emotional charges that we hold in our bodies. The CORE Technique is your tool for dealing with the incompletions. And the WONDER Technique is a wonder-ful tool for eliminating unwanted habits and conditioned responses.

We call this the WONDER Technique because the process of unplugging from a reactive behavior and letting it sink back down into nothingness is the front end of waiting for clarity. Waiting for clarity as we have just discussed is the way to make the shift from the terror of uncertainty to the wonder of uncertainty. So the WONDER technique is the starting point for helping you to make this shift and begin to live in this state of wonder.

Habits—Dismantle them rather than Replace them

One commonly proposed idea in personal development books and seminars is to change a habit by replacing one habit with a different and hopefully better one. This concept is in part based on the observation that human beings are creatures of habit. The idea of replacing one habit with another has this observation imbedded in it. There is also the assumption that because we seem to be creatures of habit this strategy is our only real option. However, there is an upgrade to this concept that is available now with the development of the Pure Awareness Techniques.

Instead of being a creature of habit—which means being the product of your conditioning—what if you developed a state of being in which you could respond spontaneously to the needs of each moment with the fullness of your Being? What if it were possible to make decisions that were not based on some prior retrained notion about what might be needed (the new habit that replaced the old one)? What if our decisions were based on a fully present, fully conscious, perfectly appropriate response to the unique needs of each moment?

Instead of being a creature of habit how about being a creature of spontaneous right action? How about becoming a person whose decisions and actions are coming directly from the infinite wisdom of the field of pure intelligence, pure knowing, the field of Pure Awareness? Now that would be a major Upgrade to your inner human software operating system!

How to do the WONDER Technique

The words for each letter of our acronym WONDER - Wait On Neutral During Extreme Reactions, describes what you actually do to use the WONDER Technique. Think of it like this. When you are about to do something that would be an expression of a habit that you want to eliminate it begins with the inception of a thought to do that thing. Nothing can happen without the thought to do it. So the mechanism is to have the thought which then leads to the action.

So the way that it works is Thought – Action.

Now for habitual thoughts the habit part gets created because we have become so skilled at doing that particular action that we have become unconsciously competent at doing it. We've become so good at it that we aren't even aware of the thought part of the formula any more.

There are four stages to the learning process, whether it is learning to ride a bike, tie our shoes or play the piano. Before we learn to do something, like tying our shoes, we don't know how to do it and someone has to do it for us. We don't even know that we can't do it. It's not even an option for us. This stage of the learning process is called *unconscious incompetence*.

At the point at which we begin to try to tie our shoes it takes a lot of concentration and effort. We may not even get it right for a while. This is the stage of learning called *conscious incompetence*. We know that we can't do it but we are practicing and working towards the next stage.

When we are successful at tying our shoes we have reached the stage called *conscious competence*. Now we know how to do it but it still takes thought and paying attention in order to do it properly.

The fourth stage of the learning process is when tying our shoes has become so familiar and we have done it so many times that we no longer have to think about it. It's as if our shoes just get tied. It's almost like they tie themselves now. It's effortless and we don't even think about it. We have now reached the fourth stage of learning which is called *unconscious competence*.

So habits are behaviors at which we have become unconsciously competent. Feeding energy into the habitual behavior is so deeply conditioned in us that we don't even realize any more that we are the ones who are feeding the thoughts and actions of the habit with energy. We have become the victims of our own unconscious competence at doing that habit.

Practice the WONDER Technique by targeting each individual habit of reactive, impulsive behavior. This may be done one habit at a time or you can make a list of all of the habits that you want to dismantle. Start noticing them and unplugging from letting energy be fed into them by default. Remember that it is you who is feeding them energy. It's just that you have become so unconsciously competent at doing the old habits that you normally don't notice that it's happening until you are already doing it. That's way they are called habits.

In order to be aware enough of the habit that you can change it, you have to have an interrupt that gives you time to make the decision to NOT feed the old thoughts and actions with energy anymore. After all, if you don't give them energy they can't manifest any more. You just have to get good at noticing the inception of the thought that is about to rear its ugly head out of nothingness and sweep you away into automatic pilot habit land.

Creating a Gap between Stimulus and Response

I remember once in the early 90's when I was waiting between flights in the Chicago O'Hare airport. I decided to browse through a book store while I was waiting. As I did one book almost literally jumped off of the shelf into my hands. It was Stephen Covey's now famous The Seven Habits of Highly Effective People. Well of course I bought it and took it with me to start reading on the plane. As I devoured this classic work I was intrigued with many of the concepts. One point that I have thought about over the years in particular that relates to our current topic was the idea that in the gap between stimulus and response we have freedom of choice. Since first reading this idea I have given it quite a lot of thought. What I have noticed is that so much of the time our actions are so quick and reactive that there isn't enough of a gap to be able to have the option of a choice. Having a gap would mean that there is an awareness, a kind of observing of what is about to happen.

The question then becomes, how can we create a big enough gap, or how can we expand and enhance our awareness of the gap between stimulus and response so that we do indeed have the freedom to chose whether or not to allow energy to flow into any given thought and turn into an action or not. This is very important because without enough awareness of a gap between stimulus and response there is no freedom of choice. You are just being the product of your learned behaviors, your conditioned responses.

So far I have discovered three ways to do this. These might be called habit interrupters. The first two are cognitive interrupters and the third which is by far the most amazingly effective one is an energetic interrupter.

Here are the classic cognitive ones which are very good:

1. Make a list.

   a. Make a list of the habits that you want to dismantle.

   b. Prioritize them and start with the one that you feel is your top priority.

   c. Consciously unplug from engaging in that habit every time it comes up.

   d. Carry a small notepad with you during the day and write down every time the habit comes up and what you did about it.

   e. Put your attention on noticing just this one habit and decide that you are going to begin to catch it earlier and earlier in the process of noticing when the thought that turns into the action of this habit is about to manifest out of the nothingness of your awareness.

   f. Making the list, choosing the highest priority habit to change and making the decision to start noticing the process of how this habit manifests from nothingness, to thought, to action, and making note of what happens each time the old habit comes up, can help to begin to create enough awareness that you can unplug the power cord and stop feeding energy into the habit.

2. Use pictures or written reminders.

   a. You already know about this one as it's commonly recommended by lots of personal development experts. You put post-it notes on your mirror. You put a note in your wallet. You put a post-it note on the side of your computer screen. You put a reminder of the habit you are changing (encoded in some way to save your privacy about it if need be) as a message on the screen saver of your computer.

b. You can use a picture of what you will be like (such as a picture of someone who is slender if your habit is over eating for example) and put it on the screensaver or on the door of your refrigerator as a habit interrupter.

c. Get creative and design or find physical reminders that will help you to notice and be more aware that you are about to engage in the old habit before you just find yourself doing it again. You get the idea.

Those are good, and here's the new one developed as a part of the emerging new field of Human Software Engineering that functions as an interrupter of conditioned responses at the deeper level of energy and information that tends to hold these habits in place.

3. Use a Human Software Engineering™ device such as the WavePod™ or WaveMaker™ or WaveMaker Pro™ to debug your inner human software and wipe out the pattern of energy that holds the habit in place.

a. The WavePod, the WaveMaker and the WaveMaker Pro are new technologies of the emerging field of Human Software Engineering (HSE). They are designed to pick up the ultra-fine electromagnetic field patterns of energy and information from the body, electronically invert them and send them back to the body via cables and "connectors" (our Human Software Engineering term for electrodes).

b. These HSE Technologies use a sophisticated application of the principle of wave interference from physics. They work in a similar but greatly expanded way to noise canceling headsets. Like a noise canceling headset, these HSE devices cancel out the wave patterns of energy but instead of canceling out the energy patterns of the noise from the environment they cancel out the energy of the "noise" of our conditioning held in our bodies.

c. The WavePod, the WaveMaker and the WaveMaker Pro represent major breakthroughs in the application of the principle of wave theory from physics to the fields of personal development, coaching, personnel development and human potential. They also have applications in health care, addiction recovery and other fields. For more information about these extraordinary new technologies see the appendix for detailed information, about applications, purchasing and training options.

d. People find that when they debug the underlying basis of the habits that they want to change that sometimes the habit just disappears. Other times the debugging opens up a much bigger gap of awareness between you and the old default habitual reaction. This means that it now becomes much, much easier to notice that the habit is about to express itself automatically and to unplug instead, shift to neutral and not allow energy to be fed into the habit. Without energy it doesn't manifest and all that is left is Pure Awareness.

Mastering the Skills of Eliminating Conditioned Responses

More on the Use of the WONDER Technique

By learning about the penetrating insights of the 12 Core Dynamics of Common Problems you can start to understand the nature of your conditioning. You'll begin to see in great detail how your preverbal conditioning caused you to make "feeling level decisions" about yourself, your relationships to people and to your experiences and interactions with the world around you. Once you understand the Core Dynamics model and become aware of specific expressions of a particular core dynamic that is causing habitual conditioned "reactive" responses, decide to become a master of these two steps:

1. Be aware of every conditioned response as it is beginning to arise in you.

2. Unplug the power/ shift to neutral.

Notice when you are beginning to react with a conditioned response as opposed to a conscious choice. You can disallow the thought to continue to receive any energy/power if you are aware of it before it launches into speech or action. The reactive conditioned thoughts are contrary to what you really want in your life. You must make the conscious choice to become aware of them. You are so used to these old habits being a part of your life that you won't tend to notice them unless you have made a decision to become aware of them. In order to catch yourself, you have to pay attention. This is where there can be a value to using the first two cognitive interrupters that are listed above.

Becoming aware of the Core Dynamic operating at the basis of your issue will help you recognize the type of conditioned responses that habitually come up in your mind. This is just like unplugging the power on a CD player or an old phonograph. It just stops or winds down.

Recognize that you are the only person who is in control of which thoughts you allow to continue to receive energy. You control which emerging thoughts are allowed to actually formulate into a fully formed thoughts and which ones you let sink back into the nothingness from which they came. This can be very powerful and liberating.

You do not have to continue to be the victim of your own thoughts. Who gives them energy anyway? It's not someone else. Thinking that you don't have control over which thoughts you allow your awareness to energize and entertain is a part of your conditioning. It is characteristic of the high level of unconscious competence that you have developed through a lifetime of energizing the habitual thoughts.

It's not true that you are a victim of your own thoughts. You just haven't known that. It is more effective to shift to neutral/unplug the power than to

- Attempt to negate the thought
- Attempt to replace the thought with another thought
- Dwell on the thought
- Deride yourself for having started to think it

One of my mentors once said, "Neutrality is the most powerful dismantler of negativity." The state of mastery of the skill of eliminating conditioned responses is when you have the very clear awareness that every action you take is coming from Pure Awareness and reactivity is absent. You know that the mastery is present when you can honestly say –

"I skillfully manage my thoughts and feelings in such a way that nothing whatsoever interferes with the fulfillment of my intentions."

When to use the WONDER Technique

- When you feel the onset of an emotional reaction

- When you notice that you are about to energize an unwanted habit

- When you feel impulsive

- This is the way that you start the technique of WAIT prior to an emotional reaction and lead directly into the CORE technique

Remembering to Use the WONDER Technique

If you follow the guidelines for creating more of a gap of awareness listed above you will basically know how to remember to use the WONDER Technique. Understand that remembering to use the WONDER Technique is by its nature a challenge because the habits are unconscious competence behaviors. That means that the only way to be truly successful is to have a realistic plan for dismantling the unconscious part of it. You will have to decide to use some combination of the habit interrupters to create the gap of awareness. Only then are the WONDER Techniques of unplugging the power cord or shifting to neutral even possible. Making the decision to adopt a plan to do this is important not only for being able to change habits that you want to change. Much more importantly, this will free you up to live from Pure Awareness more and more so that all of your actions can be the expression of who and what you really are. This is so much better a life than continuing to be the victim of your habits. It is worth the attention that it takes to do this.

How Using the WONDER Technique Can Impact Your Life

It's hard to imagine a life without all of the habits and conditioned responses that you have been inadvertently perpetuating all of your life. So, like anything else, without experiencing it you really can't know what a life like that is like. Is it worth the "work" to dismantle the old habits? Well if they are keeping you stuck in reactivity, struggle and suffering, I should say so!

What you will notice as you begin to dismantle the habits that you want to change is that there may be a period of adjustment to being non-reactive and simply not doing the things that you have done in the past. You may find yourself feeling a sense of – "But I should be doing something!" And you don't have to. If there's no clear inner directive then all that was needed in that moment was to unplug, shift to neutral and be in the WONDER of uncertainty.

You see, the WONDER Technique is really the very front end of the WAIT Technique. And while you're doing the WAIT Technique you also then do the CORE, GAP and AGAPE as you wait for clarity. So they all work together to help you re-establish your direct experience of Pure Awareness and cultivate living from Pure Awareness more and more and more. Until one day you are so grounded in Pure Awareness that you never lose the awareness of it ever again. It's a very special kind of awakening to fully know and experience that the ultimate reality of what you really are is Pure Awareness Itself and to never have this go away.

Happy unplugging!

What Keeps Us from Experiencing Pure Awareness All the Time?

It has long been thought that to live from Pure Awareness requires years and years of meditation and other spiritual and austere practices. Perhaps this was true in the past but it is also true that if you traveled by ox cart from New York to San Francisco you were lucky if you even got there not to mention how long and arduous a journey it was. Obviously the advent of new technology changes how long things take and also changes the comfort of the ride to get there. A first class seat on a 747 jet is a long way from an ox cart. Now we can get from New York to San Francisco in about five hours and even be served a lovely meal and watch your favorite movies along the way.

And so it is with the development of the Pure Awareness Techniques. They are a new technology that speeds up the process and makes the journey much more pleasant than it has ever been before. There are no difficult, arduous spiritual austerities needed. And the main thing is that we now understand the mechanics of what it is that keeps people from experiencing Pure Awareness all the time. Even more importantly we now have the new technologies needed to turn this into a first class jumbo jet ride.

The primary barriers to living from Pure Awareness all the time are the incompletions of previous painful experiences that we continue to avoid feeling throughout our life. Many people never do feel them and they take them with them to their grave. These unresolved emotional stresses and emotional pain held in our body create a kind of screen of energy between our conscious mind and the direct experience of Pure Awareness.

Meditation (which I practiced and taught for about 32 years) is a wonderful process. When practiced properly it can bring you very clear experiences of Pure Awareness. Meditation works by settling the mind down to experience Pure Awareness using a mantra (or other methods) and charms the mind inward to gradually transcend thoughts and eventually reach the experience of Pure Awareness. In the process it creates a very deep state of rest. As explained in the section on the GAP technique, when the body comes to this deep state of rest, because of the oneness of the mind and body, deep seated stresses and strains start to become neutralized. As the body relaxes they begin to "unstress" themselves. This creates activity in the body and corresponding activity in the mind that we experience as thoughts. After awhile one becomes aware that you have been thinking. This means that the activity in the body has started to lessen and the corresponding activity in the mind has begun to lessen as well. The activity of thinking no longer is fully engaging the mind. You now become aware enough that you can go back to using your mantra and again take another inward dive into Pure Awareness. This is the natural process of meditation involving an inward direction to experience Pure Awareness and an outward direction that is the natural consequence of the deep rest that occurs from settling the mind and body down into Pure Awareness.

It works and it's very pleasant. It eventually removes enough of the stresses stored in your body that it does create a state in which Pure Awareness in never lost. Prior to the Pure Awareness Techniques, a well learned and well practiced form of meditation was the best game in town for cultivating a state in which the experience of Pure Awareness is never lost.

But the thing about the Pure Awareness Techniques, in particular the CORE Technique, is that instead of gradually chipping away at the patterns of energy that create the barriers to the Awareness of Awareness we go after them in a highly targeted way. We don't just wait for them to gradually dissolve through the deep rest of meditation. We go after them.

I want to also make the distinction here between simply using the CORE Technique when you feel caught in the grip of an emotion versus using Core Dynamics Coaching and WaveMaker Coaching. Core Dynamics Coaching and WaveMaker Coaching systematically pinpoint and identify every possible barrier to living from Pure Awareness all the time. They consciously and systematically resolve each and every barrier so that we can now rapidly remove these inner obstacles to living from Pure Awareness continuously. This is a profound development. It means that we can greatly accelerate to process. What might have taken 20 or 30 years of meditation or other related practices can now be accomplished in perhaps 10 % of the time or less.

There are people who have been using Human Software Engineering, the Core Dynamics, the Pure Awareness Techniques and the WaveMaker for only two or three years and reporting that they are living and enjoying Pure Awareness all the time. It never goes away because the reality is that it is actually there all the time anyway. It's just that we are so distracted by our conditioning and we so avoid being present to life due to our unresolved emotional pain hiding just under the surface that we don't get to enjoy the presence of Pure Awareness. Those emotionally painful experiences are waiting for us to be present enough that they can come out and wave their arms at us as if to say, "Hey, I'm over here! Remember me? I'm that painful feeling that you've not wanted to feel. Come over here and complete me!"

Our conditioning of fearing being overwhelmed by those painful experiences keeps us absorbed in our activities of daily life. If the pain is really strong then we tend to absorb ourselves in even more powerful drugs than 'mere activity' so that we really don't have to feel. The avoidance of feeling emotional pain and the fear of being overwhelmed by the emotional pain are at the basis of *all* addictive behaviors. Most people are just addicted enough to their thinking and the pursuit of the fulfillment of their desires that their attention is constantly focused in an outward direction toward the objects of experience, pleasure and pain. This is just enough to keep them unaware of their own essential nature – Pure Awareness.

So it would appear that the primary thing that keeps us from experiencing Pure Awareness all the time is our database of archived incomplete emotional stresses and pains from the past that we are avoiding feeling and completing. This is why the CORE Technique is so invaluable. Finally we have a way to quickly and thoroughly resolve these incomplete experiences and remove the curtain of energy that stands in the way between Pure Awareness and our everyday normal experience of life.

What Is Life Like When You Live From Pure Awareness All The Time?

It is clear what the barriers and the reasons are that keep people from living from Pure Awareness all the time and why this state of affairs is so common in the world. But now with the development of the new technologies of Human Software Engineering anyone who wants to can very quickly begin to dismantle these barriers and live more and more from Pure Awareness until the day comes when even the illusory sense that you are an isolated individual dissolves and you awaken to the reality that you are Pure Awareness and that Pure Awareness is all there really is.

What is living in such a state like?

- You always trust and act on your intuition

- You are always true to yourself

- You feel a deep capacity for intimacy and at the same time feel totally independent and self-sufficient

- You enjoy being naturally and completely free from the influences of the past and you have no worries or concerns about the future

- You experience total presence and live fully aware and present in every moment

- You never get lost to the grip of emotion

- You experience emotions fully, much more fully and richly than ever before but you don't get lost to them

- You have a natural capacity to feel anything and everything making sensory experiences more alive and rich and full than you ever imagined were possible

- You feel a deep sense of oneness with nature and the universe

- You feel a natural alignment with and full support of all the laws of nature

- Your life feels like it is a continuous experience of being "in the Zone"

- You spontaneously function in alignment with Nature and it feels as if you are an agent of nature and the universe

- You have a profound, unshakable inner sense of peace and harmony with everything

- Life is frictionless and things happen as if by magic in ways that you could never have imagined and yet it all feels natural and perfect

- You feel a pervasive sense of permanent inner peace

- You feel completely free

- Your desires get fulfilled effortlessly and you are unattached to how and when they get fulfilled

- You have no problem with waiting when that is needed and it doesn't even feel like waiting because you are unattached to expectations, in fact you have given up the habit of creating and being attached to expectations altogether

- You feel a sense of oneness with unlimited power

- You feel unconditional love for everyone even though you still have likes and preferences

- The experience of perpetual bliss is always present

And with all of this from the outside you look just like a regular old human being just like your neighbor. Granted, when people interact with you they feel that there is something very special about you. You seem to have very clean energy. You don't seem to be bothered by anything. You have something that they want but they can't put their finger on what it is.

This is what it's like. How do I know this? Well, you remember from earlier in the book when I said that experience is the basis of true knowing and full understanding? I wouldn't have this clarity about all of this if it wasn't coming from direct experience.

But don't take my word for it. Experience it yourself. All you have to do is start using the Pure Awareness Techniques. If you want to really put booster rockets on and accelerate things even more, work with a Core Dynamics Coach or a WaveMaker Coach and go through a systematic process of debugging and upgrading your inner human software with the special intention of removing every conceivable barrier to living from Pure Awareness all the time. This can get you there even faster than just waiting for circumstances to bring up your unresolved stuff to feel into with the CORE Technique.

Now you know what is possible. Now you have the tools and techniques to remove the barriers to living from Pure Awareness all the time. It's there in the background just on the other side of your incompletions. Why not dismantle them quickly, easily and completely so that you too can enjoy a life living the continuous experience of Wholeness and Fulfillment for the rest of your life?

I hope that you will practice the Pure Awareness Techniques. And I hope that you will take advantage of the other incredible resources available to you from Great Life Technologies, LLC. Please visit our web site at www.greatlifetechnologies.com. Join our email list (which you can do at the site) so that you get our newsletters and announcements. Enjoy the other applications of Human Software Engineering and stay tuned as more and more amazing applications get developed. Check out the links in the Internet Resources section that follows. These links will guide you to detailed information about some of the many applications that are already developed as of the writing of this book.

My wish for you is that you live and enjoy the totality of who and what you really are. May you always enjoy experiencing and living from your essential nature...

pureawareness

The Five Pure Awareness Techniques And When to Use Them

1. CORE—Center Of Remaining Energy

    • Feeling into the Core of the Energy of the Feeling

    • The technique for rapidly and thoroughly completing unresolved painful experiences without suffering

    When to use CORE:

    • When you feel that you are in the grip of an emotion and want to be free of it

    • When a situation triggers the feeling of a painful experience from the past

    • While working with a Core Dynamics Coach to remove the basis of inner conflicts

2. GAP—Greater Awareness Place

    • Experiencing Pure Awareness in the Gap Between Thoughts

    • The technique for experiencing the essential nature of who and what you really are – Pure Awareness

    When to use GAP:

    • As a regular daily practice to become very familiar with the experience of Pure Awareness

    • Before doing something important to you where you would like to be operating from wholeness

    • While working with a Core Dynamics Coach to experience that you are already whole and complete

    • Any time you want to directly experience Pure Awareness

3. AGAPE—Accessing the Greater Awareness Place Everywhere

    • Experiencing Pure Awareness Everywhere

    • The technique for directly experiencing that the essential nature of who and what you are is the same as the essential nature of everything in the universe

When to use AGAPE:

- Directly following doing the GAP technique

- As a regular daily practice to directly experience that the essential nature of who and what you really are is everywhere in the universe

- Before doing something important to you where you would like to be operating from wholeness and experiencing yourself as One with everything

- Anytime that you want to experience being One with everything

4. WAIT—Waiting Allows Intuitive Truth

- Wait for clarity and only make decisions from a stable state of Pure Awareness

- The technique for being certain

When to use WAIT:

- When someone is pressuring you to make a decision such as to buy something

- Whenever you are making big decisions such as who to marry, where to live, what job to take, whether or not to start a new business

- Anytime you have doubts

- While waiting, fully feel whatever there is to be experienced. Use CORE if needed.

5. WONDER—Wait On Neutral During Extreme Reactions

- Unplugging the power cord on habitual thoughts and behaviors

- The technique for eliminating unwanted habits

When to use WONDER:

- When you feel the onset of an emotional reaction

- When you notice that you are about to energize an unwanted habit

- When you feel impulsive

- This is the way that you start the technique of WAIT

- Prior to an emotional reaction and leading directly into the CORE technique

Internet Resources

The Great Life Technologies web site: www.greatlifetechnologies.com
A rich resource of information about the many applications of Human Software Engineering

The Great Life Coaching Portal: www.greatlifecoaching.com
This is an automated scheduling system for making appointments with Coaches who have been trained and certified by Great Life Technologies to offer the wide range of Core Dynamic Coaching and WaveMaker Coaching based programs including:

- Core Dynamics Coaching

- WaveMaker Coaching

- WavePod Coaching (coming soon)

- The Peace of Mind Program (debugging the underlying stress that causes ADD/ADHD)

- The Be Smoke Free Now Program (a powerful WaveMaker and Pure Awareness Techniques based smoking cessation program that is amazingly effective for helping people easily and quickly become non-smokers for the rest of their life)

- Extraordinary Wellness Coaching – (Core Dynamics and WaveMaker based coaching for resolving the underlying inner conflicts that keep people from getting well)

- Extraordinary Relationship Coaching (resolve your resentments, improve your communication, learn to be intimate and independent both, find the ideal partner if you're single, etc.)

- Extraordinary Prosperity (our conditioning around money issues is thick and deep. Work with a Core Dynamics or WaveMaker Coach to remove all of the conditioning that gets in the way of truly prospering on all levels of your life)

- And more...

The WaveMaker Store: http://greatlifetechnologies.com/wavemakerstore.shtml
Learn about the WaveMaker, the WaveMaker Pro and the new personal debugging HSE device, the WavePod.

Articles by Tom Stone: http://greatlifetechnologies.com/articlesindex.shtml
This link is to an index of articles written by Tom Stone on various aspects of Human Software Engineering and other related topics.

Join the free Human Software Engineering Yahoo email discussion group:
http://health.groups.yahoo.com/group/HumanSoftwareEngineering/

Join the hundreds of people who are discussing Human Software Engineering in all of it many applications. Search the five years of archives with keywords for topics of interest.

Join Tom's blog for the many blog articles and the building library of blog posts about Human Software Engineering: http://greatlifetechnologies.com/Blogs/

The Peace of Mind Program:
http://greatlifetechnologies.com/PeaceOfMindQuickUpgrade.shtml

Have one of the primary underlying causes of ADD and ADHD debugged via HSE Resonance Drops which can be individualized for you and sent to you via the mail.

The Squeaky Clean Program:
http://greatlifetechnologies.com/SqueakyCleanProgram.shtml

Learn about the brilliant insights of the leading European researcher and practitioners who have been using HSE devices for decades to remove the underlying causes of chronic diseases, allergies, toxins, pathogens, etc. This is a program to get well and stay well. It is also available remotely via HSE Resonance Drops.

Core Dynamics Coach Training Options:
http://greatlifetechnologies.com/CDCTraining/Options.html

How would you like to make a great living helping people remove their inner barriers to having the life they truly want. Core Dynamics Coaching uses the Pure Awareness Techniques to resolve inner barriers faster and more completely than any other form of coaching or therapy. It's setting a new standard of coaching. This training prepares you for certification by the International Coaching Federation.

The WaveMaker Mastery Program:

http://greatlifetechnologies.com/NewMasteryProgram.html

A six month mentoring program taught by Tom Stone that not only teaches you to be a superb WaveMaker Coach but also helps you clean out your own inner barriers so that you show up as clean as possible to serve each of your coaching clients. You become someone who people want to be coached by. The get the feeling of – I'll have what she's having!

The 12 Core Dynamics of Common Problems - Audio CD set

http://greatlifetechnologies.com/CoreDynamicsCDSet.html

The 12 Core Dynamics of Common Problem two day seminar given by Tom Stone. Learn all 12 Core Dynamics insights into the nature of human conditioning and also learn the Five Pure Awareness Technique directly from Tom.